Dream
Wheeler

DEB HUNT

DEDICATION

To CC

ACKNOWLEDGMENTS

My sincere thanks to Jane for her enduring friendship over the past twenty years, and for her patience in the face of endless questions.

I want to thank Jane's friends in England, especially Pam for unearthing Jane's letters and Sally who originally transcribed them, as well as members of Jane's family, notably Annabel, Jenny, Tim and Clive. I am immensely grateful to Jane's friends and neighbours in France for always making me welcome each time I visited, especially Jeannine, Robert, Lucien, Francoise and Jean Yves. I also want to thank my agent, Pippa at Curtis Brown, whose enthusiasm for Jane's story made me believe it was a project worth pursuing. Thank you to Lisa for invaluable feedback and patient editing, to Wells Design for help with the cover and to Rachel for wizardry on the layout. And a special thank you to my partner, Clyde, whose love, support and encouragement lifted my spirits and kept me going.

AUTHOR'S NOTE

I met Jane Lambert in 1993, when she was sixty-three years old. She was trying to sell her London flat so she could move to France. I thought she was deluded, a hopeless romantic living on daydreams. How could someone so disabled think of moving to France? She had never even visited the country before, she couldn't speak the language and she had hardly any money. What's more, I thought the house she was hoping to buy looked like a derelict shack. To discover that she hoped to meet a sexy Frenchman was the final straw, confirmation that she really did have her head in the clouds.

How wrong I was. Jane Lambert is an optimistic, pragmatic adventurer willing to have a go, determined to follow her dreams no matter what the cost and prepared to risk it all for one last shot at living life to the full. She took a gutsy leap into the unknown with her eyes wide open, accepting whatever hardships might be involved, knowing the adventure would be everything, no matter what the outcome.

I've pieced together Jane's story from letters she wrote in the early days, notes on her calendars and interviews with her and her neighbours in France, as well as with friends and family in England. Inevitably I've had to fictionalise parts of the story because I wasn't there when it happened, but it's as close to the truth as I can get it. Jane has read the book and given it her seal of approval.

I hope you enjoy reading about this extraordinary woman as much as I have enjoyed writing about her.

Deb Hunt

PREFACE

Some men break your heart in two,
Some men fawn and flatter,
Some men never look at you;
And that cleans up the matter
Dorothy Parker

Summer, 1996

Jane pushed her chair towards the white plastic table on the concrete patio and reached across to shift an old pair of knickers that came in handy as a duster. She dropped the notepad she'd been carrying onto the table and wedged a pen between her frozen thumb and forefinger. Then she hesitated. She'd never put a personal ad in the paper before. She wasn't sure what to say.

Mature woman in a wheelchair looking for love? Disabled 67 year-old, wants to meet a French lover? English pensioner, enjoys oats, seeks French supplier?

The thought of ending up with a garden full of oats raised a smile but she wanted a man, not a year's supply of horse feed. In the end she kept the wording neutral.

English woman, retired and living in France, interested in fine art, music and gardening, would like to meet someone, ideally bilingual, for social outings and help reading a French newspaper.

She decided not to mention the fact that she was sixty-seven, and she left out the wheelchair too. She reasoned that people who replied to the ad should want to meet her, not her wheelchair. Besides, there was no point stacking the odds any further. Three years earlier she had moved to a sparsely populated area in a Catholic country where divorce rates were low and women outlived men by a decade or more. In France there were ten women for every seven men over the age of sixty-five. Jane was hoping to meet a widower, a divorced man or even a single man in his sixties or seventies. Younger would do (she'd never been averse to the idea of a toy boy) and it had to be someone who wasn't prejudiced against disability. The odds definitely weren't in her favour.

A cooling Atlantic breeze fluttered through the garden, lifted the fabric of Jane's orange blouse and tickled her scalp. Roses had taken root in a patch of bare earth outside the pig shed and a passion fruit vine she'd planted earlier that year had begun its long, slow climb.

She watched a fat bumblebee, its body dusted with pollen, haul its heavy cargo into the sultry air and zigzag away. The lazy buzz drifted through the silent, hot afternoon. There were no other sounds; no traffic, no radio, no planes and no distant hum of motorways, just the faint murmur of chickens in Jeannine's garden next door, squawking and scrapping as they scratched in the dirt for snails.

Trusses of blood red tomatoes, bloated by weeks of sun and rain, flourished against the concrete wall. Some were so fat and heavy their skins had split to reveal a glimpse of tender flesh inside, as though life itself was so urgent it had no choice but to burst free. Jane felt like that sometimes.

Leaning forward, she pushed a strand of dyed red hair away from her face and carefully checked the French she'd used in the advertisement before adding her phone number at the bottom of the letter in spidery script.

The metal side plates that kept her wedged into her wheelchair were hot to the touch, and her feet felt swollen inside her canvas shoes. She shifted her weight to one side and stretched her torso in an effort to find a more comfortable position. Three days of frenzied weeding, tied into her wheelchair to stop herself from falling out, had left her muscles achingly tender.

Jane reached for the letter, folded it in half and painstakingly picked at the flap of an envelope until she was able to open it and slide the letter inside.

Dropping the pen, she sat back, closed her eyes and lifted her head towards the sun, smiling in anticipation at the flood of replies she fully expected to receive.

1 MEETING JANE

Jane's two-bedroom, ground floor flat in South Ealing had been on the market for several months when I arranged to see it on a rainy day in late March 1993. The agent bent down and peered through the letterbox.

'Mrs Lambert?'

We were standing on Little Ealing Lane, a main road with nothing little about it. Cars, lorries and buses waited for the lights to change at a busy intersection further down the street, where a kebab shop and a carpet showroom jostled for space beside a newsagent and an Indian takeaway.

'It's a solid building,' the agent said, fishing in his pocket for a key. 'It's got a good layout, good bones, it's just a bit...' His voice trailed away and I was left to wonder, a bit what? He unlocked the front door, pushed it open and a long, dimly lit corridor disappeared towards the back of the house.

'Mrs Lambert?'

'Come in! I'm rather busy at the back.' A woman's high-pitched voice floated down the corridor and the agent steered me into a room on the right. 'Lets start in the living room,' he said brightly.

Cardboard boxes baggy with age littered the floor, spilling out fluffy toys, shoes, books, old vinyl records and handbags. Stacks of files were balanced on two old kitchen chairs and piles of newspaper, held together with string, leant against the wall. Black bin liners full of plastic bottles were tucked behind the sofa and an old gas fire hissed on the far wall inside an original 1960s brown tiled fireplace.

There was a television, a piano and a wall full of family photographs; smiling babies, beaming graduates, adults and children with wrinkled noses and wide grins. Shelves of books, magazines, albums, cassettes, records and more files were partially hidden behind multi coloured curtains that refused to meet across the bulging contents—collapse seemed imminent. Mounds of blue, orange and green plastic containers were stacked four feet high in places; a sea of Tupperware floating above several layers of patterned carpet.

'Ah, Mrs Lambert.'

The agent turned towards the door as a cloud of candyfloss grey hair, just visible above a salad spinner, slid towards us. Cornflower blue eyes and carmine red lips shimmered above a rainbow coloured satin top, orange trousers and blue shoes.

'Pleased to meet you,' the smiling apparition said. I waited for her to add, 'Sorry about the mess' or 'I'm having a clear out' but instead she leant forward in her red wheelchair and rummaged amongst the bin liners.

'Don't mind me,' she added, backing the chair into a tiny space beside the television to let us pass. I glanced at the agent who calmly stepped over a pile of newspaper and indicated for me to follow him.

'Shall we continue?' he said.

We walked down a long corridor, past a double bedroom, a single bedroom and a small bathroom. Everywhere I looked the house was crammed with colour. It was like walking through a life size version of Cluedo—Colonel Mustard in the living room, Miss Scarlett in the dining room. Doors and shelves were painted the colour of crushed raspberries, walls were dandelion yellow. The bathroom sported sea green tiles, an old Victorian toilet, a bright red begonia on the windowsill and wallpaper depicting pond life and water lilies. The slim kitchenette, which ran along the width of the house at the back, was painted lilac.

All I could see were anomalies. Power sockets were mounted on the wall at mid height, sinks and cabinets were lower than normal, half the cupboard doors were missing and a makeshift ramp spanned a step down as the building dropped towards the rear of the property. Every inch of available floor space was crammed with boxes, cartons and black bin liners bulging with mysterious contents. A narrow channel, just wide enough for a wheelchair, ran through the middle of it all, bordered by Tupperware.

I'd already told the agent what I was looking for: space, light and somewhere with not much work to be done. He looked understandably gloomy. 'The garden's south facing,' he added, staring out of the rain spattered window. 'Shall we have a look?'

A tea bag hung from a tree outside the back door and yellow banksia roses, rosemary, lavender, daffodils and all manner of plants I couldn't recognise vied for attention in a mad jumble against a backdrop of apple and plum trees in a plot no more than ten feet wide and twenty feet long.

'What do you think?' he asked. 'You haven't said much.'

He pushed at half a grapefruit with the toe of his shoe and I thought back to my last flat; a white box with polished floorboards, timber blinds, a handkerchief-sized lawn and a single vine. Each year I clipped it hard back to stop it getting out of control. Jane Lambert's flat was a riotous mess of colour with no central heating. It needed a new kitchen, maybe a new bathroom, and it would have to be redecorated from top to bottom. I stared at the unruly mess of a back garden and turned to the agent.

'I love it,' I said. 'I want to buy it.'

By the time we reached his office the shocked agent had recovered his composure and he shuffled through papers, searching for the details of Jane's solicitor.

'Marvellous. Great result. Wonderful potential. Good location, yes. All good. Uh, slight delay in completion, but nothing to worry about.'

'How much of a delay?'

'Well it was bought from the council…you know how it is… Thatcher's idea to stop profiteering …anyway…'

'How long is the delay?'

'Uh...let's see' He flicked through the file. 'Ah yes...five months. Nothing to worry about.'

I explained I was in no position to wait five months and I watched his pen see-saw in a rapid flutter.

'Well I don't know...Mrs Lambert might...I mean she's keen to sell...'

I gave up on the nervous solicitor and made arrangements to meet the owner at the property, in the hope we could find a solution.

'Mrs Lambert?'

'Please call me Jane. Shall we have a cuppa?'

Jane backed her wheelchair away from the front door, turned around in the entrance to the living room and scooted down the corridor. I followed to the back of the house and sat in the dining room, watching her make tea in the small lilac coloured kitchen. It was a slow, laborious process. There was a deliberation to all of Jane's movements, as if she had to force her muscles to respond; instead of gripping the kettle and lifting it, she dragged it across the counter towards her, balanced in the crook of her thumb and forefinger. The kettle wobbled in her hand as she supported one arm with the other in order to pour boiling water into cups perched on a tray on her lap. I felt an urgent need to jump up and grab the kettle.

'Can I help?'

Jane smiled and shook her head. 'No thank you.'

I made conversation while Jane finished making the tea. 'The agent told me you're moving to France.'

'Yes. The climate in France will suit me better.'

'Do you speak French?'

'I'm taking lessons at the moment. Ce nay pah tray difficeel.'

Jane had the worst French accent I'd ever heard. I sipped my tea in the sunlit dining room and said nothing. 'Hang on,' she said as she pushed her wheelchair towards a pile of papers and rummaged around, eventually producing a packet of photographs.

'Voila!' she declared, flourishing the packet. 'La maison!'

The small semi-detached house in the photographs looked sadly neglected, as if it hadn't been lived in for a long time.

'Here's the back,' she said, handing me more photographs of broken plasterwork and a rotten timber door with cracked glass. The house adjoined a badly discoloured concrete wall, which separated it from a neighbouring property.

'It's the garden I'm most excited about,' she added, handing over pictures of an empty field. It looked to be around a quarter of an acre, with a couple of stone sheds and a garage built from breezeblocks.

'It's perfect, just what I've been searching for. The land is flat, it's in a tiny hamlet so there are very few neighbours, and it's not overlooked. What more could you want?'

How about a house you can live in, I thought, and a garden instead of a field? Are you moving there on your own? How will you cope? I put down my empty cup and took a deep breath. It was none of my business. 'About the flat, I'm—

'I hope you'll be happy here.'

'The thing is I'm looking to move quickly.'

'Did the agent explain? I can't sell for another five months. I can't even exchange contracts.'

'Is that definite?'

'I'm afraid so.'

'There's no way around it? No way to speed up the process?

'No, it's an ex-council flat.'

In the early 1990s Prime Minister Margaret Thatcher embarked on a plan to encourage greater home ownership, urging council tenants across the UK to take out a mortgage and buy the flat or house they had been renting from their local authority. The incentive was a purchase price well below market value but there were conditions attached; tenants were barred from selling their newly purchased homes for at least three years—a way of discouraging instant profiteering. Jane had another five months to go before she could legally sell her flat.

'I'm sorry,' I said. 'I love the flat but I need to move sooner.'

We skirted the subject, chatted about France and French culture, found things we could laugh about to ease the looming disappointment neither of us wanted to face, and all the time Jane sat hunched in her chair. She narrowed her eyes, cupped her hands around her mug of tea and a slow, determined smile spread across her face. When her clear blue eyes met mine it felt like the sun was peeping out from behind a cloud.

'I think I've got a solution,' she said.

'You have?'

'Yes. There's a spare room. Why don't you move in?'

Several seconds elapsed as I digested what Jane had said. She was suggesting a complete stranger move in with her. She wanted us to live together, in a flat I wanted to buy but couldn't because she wasn't allowed to sell it. And we had met for the first time a week before.

The silence stretched on. I couldn't think what to say. If first impressions were anything to go by, we were polar opposites. I was in my mid thirties, the original Miss Prissy Knickers. I'd always lived alone and my world was monochromatic, neat and tidy. Jane looked to be in her early sixties, a wild child happy to exist in a state of perpetual untidiness. Colourful and fun maybe and, if I was honest, not unappealing to someone as buttoned up as I was, but where was the structure, where was the organisation in all that chaos? And where was the space for anyone else? Jane was in a wheelchair. There was barely enough room for her to squeeze past all the belongings that littered the flat. And what about the legal position? What if it went wrong?

'It won't be for long,' said Jane, warming to the idea. 'Besides, I'll be making a trip to France soon to sort out paperwork. You can have the single bedroom.' Sensing I was hesitating she pressed on. 'I might even be able to move to France earlier and leave you here.'

I was a freelance editor, producing corporate newsletters and brochures from home, long before the days of desktop publishing and digital cameras. I tried to picture myself in Jane's flat, at a desk covered in pictures, articles and page layouts. It was a messy business and I needed somewhere calm to cope. Then there was my computer, printer, filing cabinet and all the paraphernalia that went with working freelance. Jane must have read my thoughts.

'I can clear some space in the front room for you,' she said.

Was she serious? The front room with all those boxes and Tupperware and bags of plastic bottles and piles of recycled newspaper and goodness knows what else?

'I'm not sure that's such—'

'There's a fete next weekend, I've been collecting things to sell. A lot of it will go then.'

That explained the fluffy toys at least.

'I'm gradually clearing things out. Most of the furniture is being sold over the next few weeks.'

There was no reason to accept such a radical proposal, there were plenty of other properties on the market and finding somewhere else wouldn't be a problem. Yet I hesitated. It was partly the flat, which I'd fallen in love with, but there was something else. Jane was everything I wasn't, a free spirit, full of colour and fun, someone willing to embrace life, no matter how challenging the adventure might be.

I longed to let myself go in that way. If a woman in a wheelchair could be so free and easy, maybe I could too? I started to wonder if I could learn something from her then I backed away from the idea as quickly as I had considered it. It wasn't sensible. The differences between us were too great. Logic said it wouldn't work. And anyway, how would someone as disabled as Jane cope with a lodger, in a small two bedroom flat, when she was trying to pack away the past thirty years of her life?

'We can make it work,' said Jane, 'and if it doesn't we'll think of something else.'

I opened my mouth to say no, I'm really sorry but I think I'll have to keep looking. I meant to say I hope you find another buyer and good luck in France.

What I wanted to say was I'm afraid I'm not the kind of person to take that sort of risk. For some reason that's not what came out.

'Let's give it a go,' I said.

2 MOVING IN

'You're moving in with the vendor?'

'Yes.'

'You do realise that's highly irregular? You haven't exchanged contracts and there's nothing in writing. You have no kind of formal, written agreement.'

'No,' I said, bemused by my recklessness but determined to see it through.

'I must advise you, in the strongest possible terms, not to proceed on this basis.'

'We shook hands on it.'

There was a sigh of frustration from the solicitor on the other end of the line. 'I cannot condone this move. If you insist on proceeding I will **not** correspond with you at Mrs Lambert's address.'

And he never did.

One bright, clear Tuesday morning at the beginning of April I moved in with Jane. I took a single suitcase, the bare minimum of what I would need for work and Megan, a nine-year-old black and white cat I'd somehow forgotten to mention. Jane wasn't remotely fazed. 'How lovely,' she said. 'I do like cats.'

We skirted politely around each other in the first few days and I spent a lot of time outdoors. The garden fascinated me. Whatever Jane planted seemed to grow including the top of a pineapple sunk into the soil, and none of it had any chemical help. Avocado stones standing on a piece of soggy kitchen roll were encouraged to sprout on a sunny windowsill, Coffee grounds were tipped onto the compost heap or poured into pot plants. Tea bags were hurled out at random to slowly decay beneath the jungle of plants.

'They help enrich the soil,' said Jane, flinging another Tetley's out the back door.

If any proof were needed that Jane's approach worked it came one night when I stood at the back door, watching an aircraft on its final descent into Heathrow. The skyline was a smoky blur of chimneys and terraced houses, with a patchwork of small back yards below it. Most consisted of gravel or concrete pavers, with pot plants starved of nutrients.

Stretched in front of me, in stark contrast, was a slim strip of fertile soil, abundant with life and untouched by chemicals for nearly thirty years. New shoots pushed to the surface through a maze of rotting vegetation, tea bags, soggy kitchen roll, potato peelings, eggshells and upturned grapefruit; another weapon in Jane's on-going war against slugs. I heard a rustling sound at my feet and looked down. A hedgehog, the first I'd ever seen in London, was snuffling its way towards the compost heap at the bottom of the garden.

I quickly discovered that there was method in the chaos of Jane's life. The 'rubbish' I'd seen in the front room was despatched to a local adventure playground for disabled children, where Jane was a regular volunteer. Then there was the recycling. Jane threw nothing away. Long before recycling became the norm, Jane re-used everything. An old sink was used as a planter box, a disused cat flap was turned into a picture frame, torn bits of cardboard were cut into circles for a maths class, corks from wine bottles turned into boats for science experiments. Jane had only recently retired from teaching and she was still in touch with teachers.

She kept anything she thought others might find useful. In the days when greed was good and consumption king, Jane fought against the tide. She hated waste and was convinced someone would find a use for the things she couldn't bring herself to throw away.

At sixty-three, severely disabled and confined to a wheelchair, Jane never left the house without lipstick. She flirted outrageously with any man who came to the front door and refused to go to bed before midnight. She didn't hesitate to treat herself to a whisky whenever she felt like one and she refused to wear anything black. There was no surface, no article of clothing, no crockery or cutlery in the house that wasn't brightly coloured.

I found out Jane was a firm believer in astrology and the world of spirit, and she knew things the rest of us had forgotten in our love affair with cosmetics, chemicals and pharmaceuticals. Cut lemons can soften the skin on your elbows, mothballs hung in fruit trees keep pests away, there's a small frog that will eat the mosquitoes breeding inside your bromeliads and slugs love beer. Empty yogurt pots buried in the back garden were brimful of foaming beer and bloated slugs.

I envied Jane her crazy, colourful optimism and I felt bland and buttoned up by comparison. I also kept thinking how wonderful it would be once she'd gone. I'd be free to clear the house of clutter, rip up the carpets, expose the floorboards and paint everything white.

I set up my desk in the front room and concentrated on work, occasionally joining a parade of commuters heading into central London on the tube, most of us clothed in black, brown, charcoal or navy. Viewed from a distance we must have looked like the march of the living dead. As an experiment one day I mentally dressed us in Jane's clothes, transforming the zombies into a carnival of happy people. Was that why Jane surrounded herself with colour?

In the weeks that followed I learnt more about Jane's life. At the end of the Second World War she studied musical theatre at the Guildhall School of Music and Drama—a prestigious academy that counts Orlando Bloom, Daniel Craig, Ewan McGregor and Jacqueline du Pre amongst its alumni.

She had five children, one a Tupperware rep, hence the huge collection, and several grandchildren. But in all our conversations there was no mention of a husband and no mention of why she was in a wheelchair. I plucked up the courage to ask one night as we shared what felt like an illicit feast of chocolate, red wine and whisky.

'Where you ever married Jane?'

'Oh yes.'

'What happened?'

'He left, after the polio.'

'Is that why you're in a wheelchair?

Jane nodded, cradling a glass of whisky in the palm of her hand. 'At the time I thought it was flu. We had four children and I was pregnant again so I carried on doing the normal everyday things—picking up the children, pegging out the washing—and it turned out to be polio. It happened very quickly and I ended up in hospital...'

Polio epidemics caused fear and widespread panic in the late 1940s and early 1950s. The highly infectious poliovirus struck without warning, with symptoms ranging from mild, non-paralytic infection to total paralysis within a matter of hours. In its most severe form the virus reached the central nervous system, destroying the nerves responsible for muscle movement. Sufferers could wake up to find they were suddenly unable to walk and struggling to breathe.

The UK's first major outbreak was in 1947, when nearly eight thousand cases were reported. Less than five years later, fifty-eight thousand cases were reported in the US. By 1954 mass trials of a vaccine had started and it proved highly effective, reducing polio cases in the UK and US by around ninety-five per cent within six years. Jane was doubly unlucky; she caught the disease in 1956 when the number of cases had fallen rapidly, and she was also pregnant, which put her at greater risk of the virus affecting her central nervous system.

'...My husband was an actor and an opera singer. He couldn't cope with the thought of having a disabled wife so he left. It didn't put me off opera though, I still enjoy that.' She laughed. 'He ended up taking a black and white minstrel show to South Africa, at the height of apartheid. Can you believe that?'

Jane's stiffened fingers worked at the silver foil enclosing a chocolate. I realised I had finished mine and was onto my second, long before Jane had managed to remove the wrapper.

'I gave birth to my youngest son, Roger, while I was in hospital.

The local authority took all the children into care. They said I'd never recover and I wouldn't be able to look after them. My own mother said the same thing. She wrote to the authorities when I eventually came out of hospital and told them I was a terrible mother.'

Jane raised the chocolate to her mouth, her right hand supporting the weight of her left arm then she paused. 'Having children came easy,' she said. 'Getting them back was much harder.' She popped the chocolate into her mouth and chewed slowly.

'How did you manage to get them back?' I asked quietly.

'I quickly married someone else.'

My sympathy evaporated and I felt an unexpected stab of jealousy. How do you quickly marry someone else when you're in hospital, paralysed by polio? I was in my mid thirties and I'd been single all my life. I was beginning to think I'd never get married. My longest relationship had lasted two years.

'What happened to husband number two?' I asked.

'He had the grace to die early.'

I watched Jane painstakingly pick at the scrunched up chocolate wrapper, fingernail scratching and peeling the paper away from the foil. Both would be recycled.

I wondered what lay ahead for her. She was moving to what looked like a derelict shack in a remote part of north-west France, well away from the usual tourist routes. She was sixty-three, fast approaching sixty-four, confined to a wheelchair and she could barely speak the most basic French. She would be living on her own in a tiny hamlet, without any shops or services, a three hour drive from the nearest cross channel ferry port. The house she was buying hadn't been lived in for several years and it looked like it needed total renovation.

It was obvious after living with Jane for even a short time that she had very little money. Once she'd paid off her mortgage the proceeds from the sale of the flat wouldn't go far. How would she afford it? What about the cost of healthcare, repairs and maintenance, foreign taxes, insurance? Then there was the hidden cost of living away from the support of friends and family. I couldn't see how it would work.

'It's an adventure,' said Jane, correctly reading the expression on my face. Her eyes sparkled as she swirled the last of the whisky in her glass. She lifted it to her mouth, tipped her head back and drained it.

'And I love French men,' she added.

Jane had no shortage of admirers. Harris was a tall West Indian who did odd jobs around the house and who obviously adored her. There was no romance there, just straightforward adoration. The only time Harris ever refused to help was when Jane asked him to get hold of some boxes so she could start packing.

'I won't do it,' he declared. 'I don't want you to go.'

There was a French boyfriend for a while who helped when it came to practising French but he turned out to be too selfish and arrogant for Jane's liking so she dumped him and went to French classes at night school instead. I wondered how she did it. I had a string of failed relationships behind me and I envied Jane's playful approach to men.

Her flirtatious, optimistic and at times seemingly chaotic approach to life hid a steely determination that had seen Jane through extreme difficulties. She'd never wanted to live in London in the first place but she'd been hospitalised, then housed, in London. Six people, seven if you counted her second husband Geoffrey, eight including the dog, had lived in that two bedroom flat on Little Ealing Lane. There had been many times when they'd gone hungry and the kids had gone to school with cardboard patching the holes in their shoes.

Before that were the years Jane didn't like to dwell on. Four weeks in an iron lung, five years in hospital, another five in rehab, the kids in different foster homes and an unreliable husband who ran off because he couldn't cope.

Jane didn't dwell on the past. She dismissed the years of hospital and rehab and the consequent struggle to get her children back as '…a bit of a rugged time'.

Her second husband, Geoffrey, married largely to help her get the children out of care—which she managed to do, one by one—turned out to be no better than her first. He told Jane he had a farm in Hampshire, the first of many lies, and turned out to be the kind of man who promised the earth and delivered nothing. He stole from the children, pawned their belongings and spent the proceeds at the pub. When Geoffrey died, Jane and the children coped alone.

When her children were old enough to be left on their own Jane decided it was time to do something useful, so she approached a social worker to find out what work she might be suitable for. Evacuation to a girls' school in Somerset during the war hadn't taught Jane anything more useful than athletics, certainly not maths. She had a beautiful singing voice—a legacy of two years at drama school, where she developed a lifelong passion for musical theatre, opera, oratorio and grand church music—but the after effects of polio made playing a musical instrument difficult.

She decided there was no point mentioning the two years at Guildhall. That was all in the past, pre polio. She'd had a range of odd jobs, even sold encyclopaedias door to door when there was no other work and they'd needed some extra cash, but none of it seemed relevant. So when the social worker asked what qualifications or experience she had, Jane said nothing.

She started from scratch, studying for exams that got her into college where she trained as a teacher, hoping a teaching post would give her the opportunity she craved to leave London. She passed the exams, qualified as a primary school teacher and hand wrote 65 applications to schools in Somerset, Kent, Dorset, Cornwall and Gloucestershire, not easy when you can't bend your thumbs.

Each one was turned down, "…nothing to do with being disabled Mrs Lambert, you're simply not right for the post.'

Eventually she applied to a school in Brentford, just down the road from her flat in Ealing, and she went to the school in person. She wheeled into the office and handed in the application form, showing them she could talk, even if she couldn't walk.

She got the job.

3 FINANCE

The move to France was still over a year away, and Jane hadn't yet put her London flat on the market, when her phone rang one Sunday afternoon.

'Mum, guess what, you're going to inherit!'

Jane could hear the excitement in her daughter's voice. She tucked the receiver under her ear and shifted in her chair. 'Am I?' she said calmly. 'That's lovely, how do you know?'

Jane's eldest daughter, Annabel, was a flamboyant Cleopatra look-alike in her early forties, who designed jewellery and sold antiques on London's famous Portobello Road. She shared her mother's love of colour as well as her unshakeable belief in astrology and the world of spirit. The clacking sound Jane could hear on the other end of the line was Annabel, tossing her long black hair that was threaded with multi-coloured beads.

'I went to a clairvoyant! Jenny came with me and the clairvoyant said someone in the family is due to inherit. We reckon it's got to be you. She said the money's there. It's there! You just have to look for it. Isn't that marvellous news!'

Jane agreed. She had no problem believing messages from beyond the grave, but just to be sure she rang her more cautious younger daughter, Jenny, for confirmation.

'It's true,' said Jenny. 'The clairvoyant was quite insistent.'

So the following week Jane made an appointment to see her lawyer. The lawyer laughed when she heard the news and suggested she find a will first, preferably one listing her as a beneficiary. 'Try St

Catherine's House and let me know how you get on,' the bemused professional said.

In 1992 St Catherine's House on Kingsway, in the centre of London, was the official repository of all records relating to births, marriages and deaths in the UK. Jane waited patiently outside the double doors of the imposing Edwardian building while an official searched for the disabled ramp.

The only person in her family who might conceivably have left her some money was her grandfather, Pa Ferdinando. Jane's early childhood had been relatively comfortable until her father ran off when she was five years old, taking the family fortune and the Irish maid with him. He got as far as Reno in North America where he bought a quickie divorce and married the 18-year-old Irish girl. That was almost 60 years ago and he hadn't been seen or heard from since.

Jane and her mother had been plunged into poverty and anything of value was discreetly sold off to support them. Jane's mother went cap in hand to her father-in-law, Pa Ferdinando, making him promise to set up a Trust Fund for her only child—his granddaughter. The grandfather had been a wealthy man and if anyone had left Jane some money it would be him. She hoped the clairvoyant was right. If her plan to retire abroad stood any chance of success she would need all the extra cash she could get her hands on.

The official dragged the ramp out of a cupboard, slotted it into place then took a handkerchief out of his pocket and wiped his forehead with an apologetic smile.

'Sorry about that love, we don't get much call for the ramp. What can we do for you?'

'I'm looking for my grandfather's will.'

'Well, you're in the right place. Can I give you a push?'

The attendant wheeled Jane into a carpeted room lined with bookshelves. Each shelf carried hundreds of leather bound volumes and contained within each were the records of all births, marriages and deaths in the UK, dating back to 1837 when civil registrations began. The room was full of people peering at high shelves, searching through indexes and pouring over open volumes. There was an air of excitement and expectation in the hushed room.

'What was his name?'

'Ferdinando.'

'Full name?'

'We just called him Pa. Sorry, that's what everyone called him.'

'That's no good love. You'll need his full name to find him. We've got several million records in here. Mind you, Ferdinando's not that common a name.'

Jane searched in her memory for something more concrete. 'Um…it may have been George.'

'What year did he die?'

'I'm not sure about that either. It may have been around 1950.'

'You've set yourself a challenge love, haven't you? All right let's start with 1950. If you can't find him there give me a shout and we'll try a few years either side.'

The attendant disappeared into the stacks and came back carrying a large book with the year 1950 printed on the spine. He dropped the weighty volume onto a stand in front of Jane's wheelchair, the impact making the stand shudder. The book contained details of the wills of anyone with a surname beginning 'F' who had died that year in the UK.

Jane leafed through the entries. She had expected to spend hours searching but moments later she found what she was looking for. George Samuel Ferdinando, who died in the UK in 1950.

Armed with a copy of the nine page will, Jane went back to see her lawyer in Ealing. 'Success!' she declared, waving the pages as she wheeled into the office.

The lawyer laughed. 'You have my full attention Mrs Lambert.' Jane handed over the will and her lawyer read out the relevant sections. 'Here we are, grandchildren.' Jane's eyes brightened. 'When it comes to my grandchildren, if any of them are boys, I'd like them to be educated at Harrow.'

'What nonsense!' Jane said. 'The dead have no right to direct the personal lives of the living. Anyway, thank goodness I was born a girl. What else does it say?'

'It looks like…yes, there's money held in a trust fund.'

'Good. So does that mean it's protected?'

'Yes. Your generation will inherit after the death of your father.' The lawyer looked up. 'You say your father has died?' Jane did a quick mental calculation. Her father would have to be at least eighty. Given his erratic lifestyle there was every chance he was no longer alive. 'I hope so,' she beamed.

'Then you should stand to inherit. We'll contact the trust fund.'

Jane left the lawyer's office in high spirits. She was surprised the trustees hadn't tried to contact her, although when she thought more about the logistics she realised she had changed her name twice, from Ferdinando to Kavan then to Lambert. She'd also moved a couple of times since coming out of hospital, so maybe it wasn't that unusual after all. She went home and started dreaming of the fortune that lay in wait.

Three weeks later the postman delivered a letter from her lawyer. Jane leant forward in her chair, scooped up the letter from the front door mat and slipped her thumbnail under the flap of the envelope, pulling her hand backwards to break the seal. The polio that had weakened the muscles in her fingers, arms and hands, had left her thumbs permanently rigid. She tipped out two letters, one from her lawyer and one which had been forwarded from the trust fund. She eagerly scanned the contents.

'Re your letter…Ferdinando…trust fund…grandchildren …' It was the final paragraph that jumped out at her. 'We regret to inform you that Mrs Lambert is a bit in advance of the facts. Her father is still alive.'

Jane quickly drafted the trustees a reply. 'I've obviously been misinformed,' she wrote. 'Would you please convey my apologies to the family. I hope I haven't caused any distress.'

There was no indication of what she might one day stand to inherit but it was irrelevant anyway. Until her father died there would be no money.

A few days later the phone rang.

'Hello, is that Jane Lambert?' The crackle on the line suggested the woman caller was from overseas.

'Yes, speaking.'

'Well, you don't know me, but my name is Jane Ferdinando.'

The softly spoken woman laughed, simpering in a way that set Jane's nerves on edge.

'I'm married to your father,' the woman added.

Jane's heart hammered against her ribs. It had been sixty years since her father had walked out and she never expected to have anything more to do with him. She took a deep breath. 'I'm so sorry,' she said. 'I hope we haven't caused you any distress by writing.'

There was another simpering laugh. 'Oh no, not at all, you don't need to worry about that.' Jane listened in disbelief as her 'stepmom' filled in some of the gaps from the past sixty years. Her father had had three children with the eighteen-year-old Irish girl in Reno then he'd left her and married again.

'You must have missed your darling daddy all these years.'

The woman's fake 'mumsy' tone irritated Jane and she recovered her composure. 'I haven't missed him remotely,' she said. 'That man used and abused everyone his whole life, and no doubt he'll do the same to you one day. Thank you for calling. Goodbye.'

Delayed shock at the unexpected call sent tremors through her body and she gripped the arms of her wheelchair. 'You stupid man!' she shouted. 'You've been a wastrel all your life and I'm SO annoyed you're still alive!'

There was no point dwelling on the disappointment. What little money she had was tied up in the flat and it would have to be enough. It had been a struggle to raise a mortgage but property prices had soared since and Jane now had equity, for the first time in her life. Once she sold there'd be enough to pay off the mortgage and have a bit left over. That 'bit' wouldn't be much but it would have to do. The prospect of inheriting some money one day gave Jane the impetus to press on with her plans. She'd waited long enough.

After decades of interference from well-meaning social workers and officials, after two Libran husbands and three Libran headmasters—and no one loves control like a Libran—she was finally taking charge of her own life. She knew her friends were too polite to point out the obvious, that a woman in her mid sixties, confined to a wheelchair with limited movement in her arms and hands, might struggle in a new place, never mind a new country. She wasn't interested in hearing about the difficulties she would face, this was the opportunity she'd been longing for, the chance to live life the way she wanted to, answerable to no one, beholden to no one and with a world of possibility ahead. She was moving to France and nothing was going to stop her.

In the early 1990s the news was full of English people moving to France. Hordes of hungry Brits were pouring across the Channel in search of cheap second homes and it was easy to see why. The French population was falling, people were abandoning remote villages and rural properties had been left to decay. There were plenty to choose from. As property prices in England began to rise Jane calculated that if she sold her flat she might just be able to afford to buy somewhere in France and end up mortgage free. Her budget wouldn't stretch to a beautiful cottage overlooking the Loire but that didn't worry her—she didn't want to live in a popular spot—she wanted to immerse herself in another culture, far from everything she'd ever known.

In preparation for her new life abroad Jane spent months watching television programmes on French cooking, history, geography and politics. She visualised herself in France, sitting in the sunshine, learning to paint, planting a garden. And she set about finding somewhere to live.

Before computers opened a window onto the world, the only way to find a house in France was to approach individual agents. Jane took her son-in-law Tim, a sensible chap married to businesswoman Jenny, to a 'buying abroad' exhibition in Hammersmith. Agents from across France were touting glossy photographs of stone barns, ancient watermills and crumbling chateaux. Jane ignored them. She wanted a single storey house in a small village, near a town, without any English expatriates living near by. Doors and corridors in modern houses would be too narrow for her wheelchair so it would have to be an older property. It needed a front door opening onto the street, a rear entrance for the car and a large, level plot of land, preferably in a coastal region for the climate, and not too far from a cross channel ferry port.

Two weeks later a raft of property details dropped through Jane's letterbox. Daughters Annabel and Jenny spent an afternoon leafing though colourful photographs and enthusing over the descriptions.

'Oh look Mum, an old stone cottage with mature fruit trees and a river running through the back garden. You could create a pond. Think of all the jam you can make with those plums!' said the flamboyant Annabel, sitting cross-legged on the floor.

Jane's more cautious daughter Jenny had decided to indulge what she considered her mum's fantasy by playing along. 'What about this one?' she asked. 'A converted barn with a sun drenched, south facing garden. We can all come and stay for summer holidays. We'll camp in the back garden.'

'Add it to the pile for viewing,' said Jane.

Jenny smiled. 'Viewing? How will you view it?"

'I'll go to France.'

'Why would you do that?'

'How else can I decide which one to buy?'

'Are you serious?'

Jenny looked up, trying to read her mum's expression as Jane carried on leafing through details.

'Of course I'm serious. Why do you think I've been looking at property details?'

'It's a great idea Mum but it's hardly practical, is it?'

'Isn't it?'

'No!'

'We'll see,' said Jane, calmly.

'Mum, it's a daydream, we all know that.'

'I'm not daydreaming.'

Jenny took a deep breath then spoke quietly but firmly, trying to keep a lid on the rising panic she felt. 'It's a ridiculous idea Mum. You've never even been to France on *holiday*. You can't speak French and you don't know anyone who lives there. Forget it, you won't cope.'

Jane smiled and Jenny recognised the stubborn look on her mum's face.

'Mum.'

'What?'

'How are you going to get there?'

'I'm going to drive.'

4 FREEDOM

Travelling in a car with Jane can be a gut wrenching, heart stopping experience. Few people who have ever done it would willingly do it again. She can strike fear into passengers, other road users and sometimes, even pedestrians. Jane has been known to mount the pavement, drive the wrong way round a roundabout and hit the car in front, without any apparent reason, while driving in a line of traffic at maximum speed.

'How did that happen?'

'No idea Jane, shall we pull over?'

'Why is that idiot hooting? What's his problem?'

'I think you may have wandered onto his side of the road.'

'Nonsense. He just wants the whole road to himself.'

Jane is oblivious to the fear and mayhem she spreads, and in her typically generous fashion she's always happy to offer someone a lift. The most she will admit is that she doesn't like driving. Freedom has its price, she says. No car, no freedom.

Jane's second husband, Geoffrey, refused to allow her to drive, so her only means of independent transport while he was alive was a motorised three-wheeler. It was a bizarre-looking contraption, with a pram hood, a left hand control to increase speed, left and right controls for turning corners and a long tiller bar that acted as a brake. She looked like a character from a Sherlock Holmes novel. At maximum speed she could travel close to jogging pace.

When Geoffrey died Jane got her first taste of freedom, at fifty years old, with an electric trike. The trike's main drawback was that it didn't have space to carry a wheelchair; Jane had to shuffle across into the driver's seat and leave her chair behind. If she thought she might need a wheelchair when she reached her destination she would lash it to the roof of the trike with elastic bungee straps. Local children chanted as she drove past—*dah dah dah dah, dah dah dah dah, Batman!* Fully charged the trike could get Jane to Heathrow airport and back, a journey of about forty miles. It was ideal for flying kites in the local park with school children standing on the back, although that dramatically increased power consumption and meant she barely made it home from the park. One day the ubiquitous 'Man from the Ministry' called.

'How are you getting on with the trike?' he asked.

'Not bad, but I'd like to go a bit further.'

'Why don't you apply for a petrol driven vehicle? It's no more difficult to drive than that trike you've got now.'

He filled out the necessary paperwork and with a stroke of his pen Jane was let loose.

Her new car was a specially adapted three-wheeler with a fibreglass body and a motorbike engine. The driver's seat slid sideways, to allow Jane to get in and out of the car, and there was space to carry a wheelchair in the back. It had a recommended cruising speed of forty miles an hour, with a warning not to exceed fifty. Its only drawback was that it couldn't take passengers, not that many other people saw that as such a disadvantage. And because it was classed as a car Jane was allowed to travel on motorways. Like Toad of Toad Hall, she was off.

In the first week she drove one hundred and forty miles across Salisbury Plain to visit her mother, who lived in Sherbourne. She got lost, spent an inordinate amount of time negotiating a single roundabout in Salisbury and ended up parked in a field.

Next she drove one hundred and sixty miles to Shrewsbury to visit her first grandchild and broke down on the way home; the car got stuck in a hedge and Jane had to complete the journey by train, sharing the guard's van with a box of day old chicks.

Then when Jenny and Tim moved to Cardiff she drove for six hours to visit them, travelling the long way round the estuary to avoid the Severn Bridge, worried the high wind might plunge her and the vehicle into the river. And it probably would have.

The car eventually came to grief on the way to visit Annabel in the Ashdown Forest, in Sussex. Approaching traffic lights at the bottom of a modest hill Jane applied the brakes and nothing happened. She ploughed into the back of the car in front and the three-wheeler's fibreglass body was crushed beyond repair. Somehow Jane escaped unscathed.

To be fair, the accidents aren't always Jane's fault. There was the time in Chiswick when she was driving the three-wheeler past an industrial estate and a lorry pulled out in front of her. She just had time to check the road ahead was clear before swerving sharply to overtake, although not quite sharply enough. The lorry caught the back wing of her car and another fibreglass body was crumpled beyond repair.

'You idiot!' Jane shouted.

'Sorry love, didn't see you. Mind you, you were travelling, weren't you?'

'How come you couldn't see me then!'

Mechanics in the local garage had a good laugh at the idea that anyone could be 'travelling' in a three-wheeler disability vehicle. If anyone could, Jane could.

Eager to forge ahead with her French adventure Jane lined up a series of property inspections for November 1992. She was reluctant to make her first trip to France alone—and disinclined to take someone who might try to influence her—so she approached her next-door neighbour, a young out of work student who agreed to help navigate in return for an all expenses paid week in France.

It may have seemed odd that Jane wanted to inspect properties in the depths of winter but it was a deliberate move; from what she'd seen on television she was sure she would love France in summer, she wanted to find out what it would be like on a grey winter's day.

By now Jane was driving a Morris Metro, a proper car converted to use hand controls, with a box on top to store her wheelchair, and by some miracle of divine intervention (legions of spirit guides and guardian angels must have been on full alert) Jane survived her first trip to France.

She and her student navigator drove from London to Portsmouth then they took the night ferry to St Malo on the north Brittany coastline. Jane was enchanted by the countryside, thrilled at the novelty of another culture and uplifted by the music of a language that still barely made sense.

She adapted to driving on the 'wrong' side of the road, avoided collisions at junctions and roundabouts, made sense of French road signs and marvelled at the many prehistoric standing stones they passed. Armed with property details and accompanied by a local immobilier—the French equivalent of a real estate agent—they criss-crossed Morbihan in southern Brittany, stopping at Auray, St Goustan and Carnac.

Each property the estate agent showed them was utterly gorgeous and totally unsuitable. One captivating 'longere' offered a steeply sloping garden, damp problems, inadequate heating and a higher than expected price. It was also too far from the coast.

They drove on, plunging deep into the French countryside in search of the perfect property, passing under the arches of an ancient prison at Hennebon. Converted farmhouses, granite barns and ruined cottages were crossed off the list one by one. Damp problems, lack of heating, an external staircase, a gravel drive, a sloping garden, narrow corridors; they all had something that made them unsuitable for someone in a wheelchair. At the end of the week Jane drove home exhausted and bitterly disappointed.

'How did you get on Mum?' Jenny asked.

'I'll have to go over again.'

Jenny was relieved and hoped the project would quietly be forgotten. Jane was more determined than ever.

She made arrangements to go again the following year, in February 1993, this time with her good friend Pam, a peripatetic music teacher originally from the North of England. A petite woman with big eyes and wavy brown hair, Pam's small frame housed a much larger personality. She was a straight talking, no nonsense Northerner.

They first met when Pam was asked to play the piano during the weekly music lessons at the primary school in Brentford where Jane worked. Jane had a beautiful singing voice but the after effects of polio made accompaniment difficult. Pam stepped in to help and in the common room afterwards they discovered a shared love of fine art, gardening and classical music.

'I'd love to go to concerts,' said Jane. 'The only problem is I'm not allowed in without a chaperone.'

'You've just found one,' Pam replied.

They went everywhere together, to the Royal Festival Hall, the Royal Opera House, art galleries, museums and concert halls. In doing so they developed a lasting friendship. When Jane declared, 'I'm going to retire to France and paint,' Pam didn't doubt it. In her opinion, moving across the Channel wouldn't daunt someone who'd been trapped inside an iron lung six weeks before she gave birth. 'Good for you,' was all she said.

Jane knew Pam would tell her exactly what she thought of any potential property they looked at and her straight-talking friend wouldn't get carried away by any romantic notions of what it might be like to live in France either.

Their target areas this time were further south, La Vendee and Loire Atlantique, two 'départements' side by side on the southern edge of Brittany, bordered by the Atlantic Ocean. Jane drove from London to Calais, Pam on high alert beside her, and Pam tried to do most of the driving in France, navigating their way around Paris in the early morning fog. When she wasn't behind the wheel Pam kept watch.

'Jane, wake up!'

'What?'

'You were nodding off.'

'Oh don't be ridiculous, of course I wasn't.' Jane sat a little straighter and gripped the wheel.

Northern France was going through an unseasonable heat wave that year. Still officially winter, temperatures had soared above twenty degrees and the sun shone every day. In spite of the encouraging weather the perfect property was still no closer.

In La Vendée they looked at a house with large holes in the floor, a roofline that sagged and ivy growing inside. In Champs St Pere, a pretty village near the coast with a regular market, a bank, a post office and a pharmacy, Jane found a 'sensible' house with high ceilings, a decent sized garage and oil-fired central heating. It had no atmosphere, the gravel drive was a problem and so was the small factory at the end of the garden, but it had to be considered a candidate. They kept driving.

A fully furnished bungalow, full of heavy carved Breton furniture, was rejected because the path at the side sloped too steeply. Another was turned down when the owner proudly declared, 'Il y a beaucoup d'anglais ici.' Living next door to lots of English people wasn't what Jane wanted.

Still in La Vendée, a retired couple showed them around a house on a main road. It had the necessary 'ambience', a garden full of roses and fruit trees and a poodle who adored visitors, but it also had a sloping concrete drive, a garage not lofty enough for the chair hoist, shallow steps at every door into the garden and, worst of all, a noticeable damp patch on the ceiling.

'Ah, ne vous inquietez pas. That is not a problem,' said the owner, handing them a glass of home made rose wine. 'It is just coming from the roof.'

Then came a small house next to a forgotten railway line. Six trains a day ran on the single branch line and there wasn't another house to be seen for miles. It had running water, electricity, good drainage and a beautiful garden. Jane was captivated. She had finally found what she'd been searching for. It looked like a patch of paradise, and the prospect of a slow train rumbling past several times a day only added to its charm. Pam wasn't convinced.

'It's a bit isolated Jane,' she said.

The next day they drove towards St Nazaire, in Loire-Atlantique. Some people call it the forgotten end of the Loire Valley. Others call it the ugly end. There are no grand chateaux and sweeping vineyards, no neat villages of honeyed stone and no fields of sunflowers shifting in the wind. Loire Atlantique is a different prospect altogether. It's an area marked by white salt pans, industrial shipbuilding and oil refineries. In places, flat swamps and boggy marshland stretch as far as the eye can see. Look closer and there are ancient forests, slow moving rivers, vast collections of prehistoric standing stones and a coastline of rocky beauty.

As a child during the war, forbidden to speak when news bulletins were on the radio, Jane had heard the name St Nazaire. They were visiting for no other reason than that it had stuck in her memory. The name Donges was different. En route to St Nazaire Jane kept seeing it on signposts and sensed it had significance, although she had no idea why.

It was a dispiriting day. Several properties they'd arranged to view were in the commune of Donges and all were unsuitable, some needed major modifications, others were nearing collapse. Jane didn't even bother to get out of the car in one place. She shook her head and the frustrated agent frowned.

'Why?' he asked.

Jane pointed at the cluster of well-managed houses.

'Too many people,' she said. 'It's too tidy.'

After dozens of viewings, hundreds of kilometres of driving and four nights in France, each in a different hotel, Jane could barely summon the energy to view the last house on the list. She wasn't the only one who'd had enough. The agent gave her the address of the final property.

'Let me know if you like it, I can come back in the morning with a key,' he said, clearly not expecting to hear back.

They drove towards the small town of Donges, looking for the even smaller hamlet of Maca, too small to be called a village. The towering stacks of an oil refinery marked the turn off from the main road. There was no village centre, no café, no patisserie selling butter rich croissants or boulangerie for freshly baked baguettes. There wasn't even a church. Maca had just one road in, and another road out, with a narrow side turning that disappeared over a hillside into the distance. It consisted of a dozen houses along a single road.

This was the rural France most tourists never see. The people who lived here, and who had lived her for generations, liked to be left alone.

5 FIELD OF DREAMS

Jane pulled up outside a small, single storey, semi-detached house facing the main road. Faded green paint was peeling from the half glazed front door and above it, tucked hard against the shallow pitched roof, was a tiny closed shutter, less than half a metre square, behind a simple wrought iron panel. Squeezed to the right of the front door was a slim window and beside it a modest outhouse that looked derelict. An unfenced patch of garden, straggly with weeds, led straight onto the road. The house was attached to a neighbouring property on its left and on the right was a small side road, which rose over a wooded hillside and disappeared into the distance.

'Come on, we've just got time before it gets dark,' said Pam.

Jane was exhausted. Getting in and out of the car was a physically demanding procedure and she'd had enough. 'Pam, you know what I'm looking for. If you think it's OK I'll have a look, otherwise let's leave it,' she said.

Pam got out of the car and walked towards the empty house. Jane watched her friend cross the scrub of front garden and peer through a grubby window. It didn't look up to much on the outside and she doubted if it would be worth seeing inside. Her mind was set on the railway cottage and this little place looked nothing by comparison. She watched Pam press her nose against the glass, cupping her hands to block out the light.

'It's a bit scruffy,' Pam called.

'What's it like at the back?'

'I'll have a look.'

Pam walked around the side of the house and re-appeared moments later. 'You have to see this,' she called, grinning broadly. 'This will knock your socks off!'

Jane sighed and started the procedure she'd gone through thousands of times before. She opened the driver's door then, with the engine still running, she flicked a switch on the dashboard. A large box lying on the roof of the car slid sideways and tipped up until it was vertical. The bottom edge swung open and her folded up wheelchair could just be seen inside. She flicked the switch again and the bright red wheelchair slowly descended, suspended on a rope with a large metal bar at the end of it, which was hooked under the seat. The chair swung against the side of the car on its descent and Jane reached out to steady it.

Once it was safely on the ground she released the hook, flicked the switch again and watched the rope slowly rise towards the box. When it reached the top she flicked the switch again to tip the box into a horizontal position and retract it onto the roof. Only then could she switch off the engine. Reaching sideways she shook the chair open with one hand and applied the brakes.

Next she reached inside the well of the passenger seat for a sheet of hard plastic and jammed it under her bottom, bridging the divide between her car seat and the wheelchair. She wriggled across the plastic, gripping the wheel to steady herself as she settled into her chair then she withdrew the plastic and threw it back into the car.

She fished out the side panels and the footplates for the wheelchair, which were stored behind the driver's seat, and slotted each one into place. She then picked up her legs, placed them on the footplates and reached in to retrieve the keys. Finally she wheeled backwards to give herself enough room to swing the car door shut.

'Right, let's have a look.'

Pam grabbed the handles of Jane's chair and pushed it around the side of the house. When the back garden came into view Jane sat up in her chair.

'That's...wow!'

'I thought you'd say that.'

Jane scanned the large plot of land. It backed onto a field, which led to the wooded hillside. The neighbouring house was hidden behind a concrete wall and the garden bordered the side road. It wasn't overlooked by anyone.

'That would make a magnificent garden.'

For now the 'garden' was a patch of grassland peppered with early dandelions. A stand of pampas grass and a couple of old rose bushes were all that identified it as a garden and not a field. A derelict barn stood in the far left corner, an old animal shed in the far right and another couple of outbuildings, one a crumbling pig sty, bordered the road. The outbuildings ran almost the entire length of the right hand edge of the plot, giving privacy from the road. There was just enough space on that side of the garden to drive a car off the road and park it, on a small patch of concrete, near the back veranda.

Jane hadn't missed the rotten timber door to one side of the house, the plastic roof on the veranda that probably leaked and a metal door that would be heavy and difficult to open. It wasn't any worse than others they'd seen. The house needed work but the plot was level. That counted for a lot. A tiny attic window, tucked into the loft where grain would once have been stored, might indicate a usable space, which could mean somewhere for guests to stay. The house had possibilities, definite possibilities.

They checked into a local hotel and arranged to meet the agent the next morning.

Once inside the house, it came as no surprise to learn that it hadn't been lived in for seven years. Window frames were grimy with black mould and the house had been badly neglected. It had a small living room with a boarded up fireplace, two bedrooms and a tiny kitchen that consisted of nothing but a stone sink—there were no cabinets and no appliances. There was no bathroom either; the only toilet was in a small hut at the top of the garden, next to the old animal shed. Plaster crumbled from the walls in the annexe to one side of the house, and the door leading into it was riddled with rot.

Pam climbed the stairs to have a look at the loft and reported daylight shining through the roof.

'It would need a lot of work before anyone could sleep up there,' she said.

Jane nodded, seeing nothing but potential. 'I could move that door,' she said, indicating the door to the annexe. 'And the bedroom's not too bad. I could turn the second bedroom into a kitchen, and that annexe would make a great living room,' she added, warming to the theme.

All the time her attention kept being drawn back to the magnificent plot of land at the back of the house. Pam shook her head. In her opinion it was a damp, smelly hovel.

The drive back to Calais involved an overnight stop in Rouen, the historic capital city of Normandy, where they struggled with road repairs, detours and one-way traffic. They found the Cathedral, not as Monet depicted it but smothered in scaffolding and too cold inside to appreciate its beauty. The next day, barely ten kilometres from the centre of Calais, they juddered to a halt at the side of the road. Pam got out and found the tyre on the front nearside wheel in ribbons. She rummaged in the boot for Jane's emergency triangle, slotted it into place and stood it on the road, quickly attracting the attention of another car with GB plates.

'He hasn't got time to change the tyre but he can give me a lift to the port or take a message for help,' Pam said, 'I think it's better if I stay with you and let him take a message, don't you?'

'Yes. Hang on, I'll write a note in case he doesn't speak French.'

Jane fished around in the car for a scrap of paper and a pen. The hard fought gains of months spent studying French at night school counted for nothing as her French vocabulary vanished and a black hole swallowed any intelligent translation of 'disabled'. Jane could get no further than, 'Il y a une femme…'

'He's keen to get going Jane.'

'Just a minute.' Jane hastily scribbled on the note, handed it over and they settled down to wait for help to arrive. The wait was long enough for Jane to reconsider what she'd written and a smile spread across her face. Her shoulders lifted and she started to shake with laughter.

'What on earth's the matter?' asked Pam.

Jane wiped her eyes. 'I couldn't think of the word for disabled. I wrote deshabille. I think I just told him there's a naked woman on the side of the road—and she needs help!'

Before the promised help could arrive an English delivery driver stopped. 'I can't change the tyre I've got a bad back, but I can take a message if you like.' His innocent remark sent Jane into a renewed fit of giggles. 'No thanks,' she said, 'we tried that.' Next to stop was an agent for one of the ferry companies, dressed in an immaculate suit and reluctant to get his hands dirty. The eventual hero was a British lorry driver, who found the jack and spare in the boot and changed the wheel in ten minutes.

'There you go love, bon voyage.'

Jane's children wasted no time telling their mum exactly what they thought. Jenny, the sensible businesswoman who'd encouraged her mum at first, thinking it was a whim that would pass, was hysterical. 'It's the most ridiculous idea I've ever heard. What happens if you get sick? Who will help you? How will you cope? What if you have an accident? You'll be entirely on your own!'

'Jenny, I've always wanted to get away from London and live in the country, you know that.'

'But why France? Why so far away?'

'Because I can't afford to buy anywhere in England. I thought about the Netherlands but the climate's not so good. There's plenty of space in France and properties are affordable. And it's warmer there. Oh come on Jenny, France is easy to get to, you'll be able to visit.'

'Have you done a budget? Have you worked out what it will cost?'

Jenny's fears weren't unfounded. When Jane had worked as a volunteer at the Log Cabin, a local adventure playground run to help disadvantaged children, she suggested they set up a train ride at the annual fete, which always brought in valuable revenue for the charity. Jane assumed the rides would do the same. She was right in thinking children would love the train, and it's cheerful conductor, but she hadn't fully calculated the expense involved. When they came to reconcile the budget, the train equipment hire costs outweighed the entire fete's profits for that year.

'I'll manage,' said Jane.

Jane's youngest son, Roger, a slim, wiry lad in his late thirties, struggled to understand why his mum would want to live in a country where she couldn't speak the language. 'What about street signs, application forms, instruction manuals, what about television and newspapers, how will you read them? How will you talk to doctors or dentists? How Mum?'

'I'll learn,' said Jane.

Jane's other daughter, Nicky—Jenny's twin sister—already lived overseas so she wasn't so concerned about her mum moving to France. Jane's oldest children, Clive and Annabel, were more supportive. Clive was an eccentric giant of a man in his mid forties with a long ponytail, a bushy beard and an intellect and curiosity about the world that matched his size. As a seven year old, in answer to the question 'What will you be when you grow up?' Clive solemnly declared he was going to be a genius. He was saved from pomposity by a silly sense of humour. An electronic engineer by trade and a keen amateur astrologer, Clive saw nothing wrong in his mum moving to France.

'It's up to you,' he said. 'I reckon you're old enough to make up your own mind.'

'It's Karma,' said Annabel, the colourful Cleopatra look-alike. 'Go for it Mum.'

Ultimately, it was up to Jane. She didn't doubt she wanted to move but had she found the right house? With a late night glass of whisky she made a list of four possible properties and gave each one a score based on access, location, work to be done, future potential and distance to a ferry port. Each had its merits but the railway cottage came out a clear winner. It had everything Jane wanted, it didn't need much work and it looked gorgeous.

The only drawback was its location; the nearest neighbour was miles away, but so what? She wanted isolation. She craved a quiet life. It was a rural idyll where she could paint and create a garden. It was perfect. Or was it?

Jane forced herself to consider her daughter Jenny's reservations. What if she fell out of her wheelchair? What if she got stuck trying to manoeuvre in or out of the car? What if she locked herself out? These were all things that had happened more than once. She thought about the difficulties she might face, on her own, without any neighbours. Maybe Jenny had a point. If she had an accident in the railway cottage no one would hear her call for help. Reluctantly she accepted she might be better off living closer to other people and she struck the railway cottage off the list.

At the end of the night the house at the top of her list, the one with most points, was the derelict cottage in Maca, deep in the rural French département of Donges.

Jane arranged to send a holding deposit and she contacted the agent to explain there would be a delay in completion of at least six months. *I have to sell my flat,* she wrote. The agent's reply reassured her. *Don't worry Madame Lambert. The house has been empty for many years, Monsieur and Madame La Gueux are happy to wait.* Jane hoped he was right.

She put her London flat on the market and waited for a buyer. I was a long time coming. As the weeks dragged on Jane started to lose her nerve. What if someone else saw the house in Maca and put in an offer? What if they found a cash buyer? She couldn't bear to go through that exhausting search again. A bridging loan might help—it would be expensive, but no more costly than losing the house and starting again. She phoned her bank manager and made an appointment.

A few days later Jane received a phone call.

'Mum, it's Clive. Do you remember Annette?'

Annette was Clive's ex-girlfriend, a woman Jane had got on well with. She'd been sorry when Clive and Annette had split up and even sorrier when they'd lost touch altogether. It had been a couple of years since either of them heard from Annette.

'Yes of course I remember Annette, have you heard from her? How is she?'

'She rang me at seven o'clock this morning. She's moved to Athens and she's working as a professional medium. She said she had an urgent message for you.'

'For me?'

'Yes I know, it's weird isn't it. She said it was from the grandfather with the tight purse strings.'

Jane held the phone closer to her ear as a tingle of anticipation ran across her scalp. Her grandfather—Pa Ferdinando—was the man she was hoping one day to inherit from. He'd been exceptionally careful with money and was known in the family as 'the man with the tight purse strings.'

'What was the message?'

'Annette knew you were moving, I've got no idea how. She said you mustn't try to rush things. She said let time take its natural course, or something like that. I don't understand what she's talking about. Do you?'

Jane knew exactly what 'Pa' was trying to tell her and she was staggered at the accuracy of the message. 'Pa' didn't think the bridging loan was such a good idea. Jane decided there was no point questioning his wisdom, even if it did come from beyond the grave. It was good advice. What if the flat didn't sell? What if she got into trouble and couldn't repay the loan?

She cancelled the appointment with the bank and waited patiently for the sale of her flat to go through.

6 ALLEZ EN ROUTE!

As soon as her three-year compulsory wait to sell the flat was over—four months after I moved in—Jane left for France. It was August 1993, the day after her sixty-fourth birthday.

'It's a good omen,' said the optimistic Annabel, who was joining her mum for the drive over to France. I helped Annabel cram the last few bags into the back of Jane's car, already weighed down with plants from the garden, bedding, books, clothes, photographs and the inevitable Tupperware.

With no money for a professional removal firm Jane's two sons, Clive and Roger, along with Roger's wife Eve, were planning to follow two days later in a transit van carrying kitchen equipment, a small fridge, a sofa, a double bed, a child's bed, a television, video recorder, dining room table and two futons for guests. Jane had sold or given away the rest of her belongings and she was only taking the basic essentials to start her new life in France. It didn't look like much. At least Jane's French had improved, even if her accent did still sound like she was a high-ranking member of the British Raj.

Eyes wide with anticipation Jane pulled into the stream of traffic on Little Ealing Lane for the last time. A small crowd of friends and neighbours had gathered to see her off.

'Cheerio,' she called, waving out of the window and beaming her one hundred watt smile. 'Oh re-vwa!'

Holidaymakers had booked all the passages to St Malo, the nearest port in Brittany, so Jane and Annabel were forced to sail overnight from Portsmouth to Caen, on the Normandy coastline. It meant three hundred kilometres of driving in England and at least the same again in France, a long, tiring slog through the northwest then south towards Laval, Nantes and on to St Nazaire.

Jane didn't care. She'd survived the exhausting process of selling her flat, she'd sorted through thirty years of furniture and personal effects, reassured those who worried and ignored those who said it would never work. After months of searching for somewhere to buy, after endless worries about finance and wrangles over paperwork, her French adventure was finally underway. She was heading for a new life.

The euphoria she felt at being back in France lifted her flagging spirits. She relished the warm breeze that caressed her skin through the open window and turned her face towards the sun.

'Careful Mum, you're on the wrong side of the road.'

Jane glanced at her daughter's anxious face. Her first trip to France had been tricky and she'd occasionally felt blind-sided by the confusion of driving on the opposite side of the road, but that was six months ago. She was confident driving on the right now.

'It's all right Annabel,' she said.

'Mum it's a roundabout!'

'I know that Annabel but—

'Mum!'

Annabel grabbed the wheel and steered her mum's car away from a stream of oncoming traffic.

Jane and her daughter arrived on the outskirts of Maca in early afternoon. They drove through the tiny hamlet past a handful of houses lining the main street and pulled up outside Jane's new home. Apart from the August sunshine that lit up the front garden and the weeds that had sprung up in the intervening months, the house looked exactly as she'd seen it last, which was probably how it had looked for decades.

Jane could sense eyes watching her as she sat in the car and lowered her chair. For now they were hidden behind net curtains and heavy shutters, but there was no doubt the locals were curious to find out who was moving in.

Annabel waited on the street while her mum shifted across into her wheelchair. Dressed in a full length red skirt and loose-fitting multi-coloured top—with her black hair beaded and braided and scooped back from her face—Annabel was an obvious target for twitching curtains. And by the time Jane had finished the complicated manoeuvre she had to go through in order to extricate herself from the car, neighbouring curtains were positively shaking.

Jane wheeled her chair across the uneven gravel surface and unlocked the glazed front door, pushing it open towards the dark, musty interior. The heat of that August afternoon fingered its way in, dispelling the gloom. Rays of sunlight lit up the motes of dust that seemed to dance a welcome, before drifting back down into dense, choking piles. The lip on the sill was too high for a wheelchair so Jane made her way around the side of the house, past the entrance to the breezeblock extension with its tin roof and dirt floor, and she unlocked the metal back door.

The door opened onto a skinny veranda, the start of a basic extension that spanned half the width of the house. The threadbare, sunny veranda, with a roof made of corrugated plastic, led to a small, bare kitchen, empty save for a stone sink which was mounted at the wrong height for Jane to reach. Half way along the extension was the original back door, opening directly onto the living room in the earliest part of the house. This was a simple oblong, around thirty feet long and fifteen feet wide. One half formed the living room, the other half two bedrooms.

Jane felt a bit like Alice in Wonderland as she surveyed six doors opening from the living room. There were doors into each bedroom, a door onto the front garden, a door into the cupboard under the stairs and the original back door that now led into the extension. Three steps in one corner of the room led to a final door that concealed a staircase, which corkscrewed its way up towards the grain loft. The only other fixture in the living room was a fireplace that had been boarded up years before.

'Where's the bathroom?' Annabel asked.

'There isn't one,' Jane replied. 'There's a loo in the garden. I'm going to turn that old kitchen into a bathroom then the second bedroom can be a kitchen. If I knock through into the living room it will make a lovely big kitchen diner.'

'Then you'll only have one bedroom.'

'Yes, but go and look upstairs.'

Annabel opened the door that led to the attic, pushing away heavy cobwebs that stretched, released their hold then drifted free as the door swung open. Jane had never been up—it was too narrow for her chair to be carried up—but she'd seen the pictures.

'Pam said there was plenty of room for guests to sleep up there,' she said.

Annabel climbed the narrow staircase, which turned a tight semi-circle and led to an attic; a vast open space that spanned the entire width and length of the house. Traditionally used to store grain, it was now empty and full of cobwebs. Heavy timber beams held the roof up and daylight filtered through the broken tiles. Annabel came back down.

'There's heaps of space up there Mum but there's a large hole in the roof.'

'Never mind, that can be fixed,' Jane called.

Compared to the rest of the house the bedroom Jane planned to use wasn't in bad shape, although at just nine feet by six it was snug. There'd be enough room for a double bed, pushed hard against the wall under the window, with space beside it for a hanging rail and Jane's wheelchair. There was no point in Jane having a wardrobe, it took too long to open and close the doors.

'Look at this Mum.'

'What?'

'That window's broken, and there's a hole in the wall below it.' Annabel squatted on her hands and knees to examine the round hole. 'It looks like a bullet hole,' she said.

Jane laughed. 'Has someone been shooting at us?' They looked across the veranda and both spotted it at the same time—a circular indentation on the opposite wall, where a chasseur's bullet had left its mark; hunting must have been a favourite pastime for someone in the village.

'What's next door?' asked Annabel, brushing dirt from her knees as she stood up.

'A sort of store room, I thought it could be a sitting room one day.'

Annabel went outside and pushed open the rotting timber door that led into the breezeblock extension. Splintered wood snagged the frame and the smell of loamy earth rose from the dirt floor. In the gloom she could see plaster peeling off the damp walls and a long bench on one side of the room. It was the kind of place the Resistance might have used during the war.

Annabel came back out and stood in the garden. She breathed in the fresh air, took in the empty field, the crumbling stone barn with an old cider press just visible inside, the animal shed, the pigsty and the little *cabine* for storage. Apart from a stand of pampas grass the only plants struggling to survive in the parched, empty field were two old roses, planted near the sceptic tank.

'No mains sewage then?' she said to her mum, who had wheeled out to join her.

'No, I'll have to find out how that works.'

'There's a lot of work to do Mum.'

'I know,' Jane said. 'The builders are starting work Monday morning.'

Annabel scanned the garden and turned to look back at the house. 'There are good vibes Mum. You've done well.'

For all her independence, Jane was glad someone else shared her enthusiasm. She and Annabel unloaded the car and drove to the local Campanile Hotel for the night.

Formal contracts on the house were signed the next day, Friday, and the vanload of furniture arrived on Saturday. Clive, Roger, Eve and Annabel helped unload the van and, since building work was due to start two days later, they stored most of the furniture in the animal shed at the top of the garden.

'This will make a good garage one day,' said Jane.

Roger and Eve said nothing. It was the first time they'd seen the house and their faces betrayed their shock at discovering just how basic it was. They helped make up a futon bed in one of the downstairs rooms, so Jane would at least have somewhere to sleep, and when the unloading was finished they all went back to the hotel.

The atmosphere in the hotel restaurant that night was subdued.

'Mum, are you sure about this?' ventured Roger, her youngest son. 'The house, I mean…it's so…'

'What does coquilles mean?' Jane asked. 'Does anyone know?'

'Mum, you can't even read the menu!'

Jane put the menu down and looked at the anxious expression on her youngest son's face.

'Roger, I'm sure,' she said firmly.

'Mum knows what she's doing, don't worry,' said Annabel.

Jane hoped her daughter was right.

She saw her children off at 5.30 the next morning, ate a leisurely breakfast in the hotel, packed her overnight things into the car and drove home.

Home. It was hardly that yet. It wasn't much more than a shell with none of the basic amenities. She'd bought a house with no water, no electricity, no kitchen and no bathroom. Until building work got underway she'd have to rely on a torch, snack food, bottled water and wet wipes. Worse still, while they'd been unpacking her few belongings the day before, she discovered that her wheelchair was too wide for the hut in the garden. If she wanted the loo she'd have to use the commode she'd brought with her, either that or a bucket.

She suppressed the panic that fluttered in the base of her stomach and concentrated on the road ahead. An old nursery rhyme entered her mind as she drove towards Maca. *Monday's child is fair of face,*

Tuesday's child is full of grace...and Saturday's child works hard for a living.
That would be right. She had been born on a Saturday. There was
plenty of work ahead but it was work she was willing to tackle. The
move to France represented everything she'd been longing for—
freedom and adventure, the chance to start a new life, and who
knows? Maybe one day a new lover.

She parked her car at the back of the house, released the
wheelchair and watched a lizard basking in the sunshine as she waited
for the hoist to lower her chair to the ground. The sound of birdsong
was everywhere—blackbirds, song thrushes, sparrows, marsh tits and
reed warblers; even a pheasant flew into the garden. A line of
swallows, perched on the telephone wires, were poised in preparation
for their long flight to Africa.

Jane turned her attention to the house. It was comforting to know
that builders would be starting work the next day. She and her son
Clive had visited Maca in June to measure up and meet the agent,
who introduced them to the maitre d'oeuvre, the project manager on
whom it all hinged. He was arranging for essential repairs to happen
as soon as Jane arrived; without them, the house would be
uninhabitable.

'Tout va s'arranger Madame Lambert,' he had said. 'It will all be
arranged. Ne vous inquietez pas.' But Jane *was* worried, in spite of his
easy reassurance.

'Electricity, ca va?

'Oh oui, pas de problème.'

'Plumbing, ca va?'

'Mais oui! Pas de problème.'

Jane wheeled into the house and began moving bags and boxes.
She shifted plants into the shade and made a note to get more bottled
water. The August heat pressed close and she worked slowly—she
had no choice. It was early evening before she thought to stop for
something to eat. Scoffing the remains of a sort of sandwich left over
from breakfast and downing a can of beer in the garden, she sat and
watched a display of bats and moths flit through the twilight. She was

ready for an early night. If French workmen were anything like their English counterparts they'd be knocking on the door at 7am.

By nine o'clock the next morning, when there was still no sign of the builders, Jane drove into St Nazaire to find the agent. A manicured young receptionist looked up as she pushed her chair into the office.

'Bonjour Madame!' she chirruped.

'Bonjour Mademoiselle. I am Madame Lambert. I'm waiting—j'attends les ouvriers—the workers.'

'Ah oui Madame.' The receptionist smiled broadly. 'It is the holidays,' she said. The lack of comprehension must have shown on Jane's face. 'The workmen, they do not work in August,' she added, her smile unfaltering.

Jane felt a flutter of unease. 'But I telephoned. I said, can work begin today, August twenty-third? I was told yes, it can.'

The young receptionist smiled again, her head tilted to one side. 'I am sorry Madame Lambert. Le patron, he will be in the office after ten o'clock. Perhaps you could telephone?' She gave a sympathetic shrug of her shoulders, indicating there was no other option. Jane pictured herself living in a house with no kitchen and no bathroom for the next two weeks.

'Ou est McDonalds?' She asked.

'Comment?'

'Le restaurant Américain. McDonalds?'

'Ah, you must drive to Trignac, at thirteen kilometres.'

'Merci Mademoiselle.'

Whatever the food was like at least they'd have a disabled loo and she could get a cup of tea. After a quick stop at McDonalds Jane drove to Auchan, the nearest local supermarket, for a phone card and the basics—bread, cheese, salad, fruit and bottled water. It was gone 10am by the time she found a phone, which, like most public phone boxes, was too high for her to reach. She parked her wheelchair next to it and waited until a passer by offered to insert the card and dial the number for her. Le Patron answered the phone himself.

'Allo?'

'Bonjour, c'est Madame Lambert.'

'Ah, bonjour Madame, ca va?'

'You said the workmen could start today.'

The pause was long enough for Jane to picture the maitre raising his hands and shrugging his shoulders at the other end of the phone. When he spoke he sounded reproachful.

'Mais non, you must have misunderstood Madame, no-one works in August. But do not worry, I will come and see you this afternoon.'

He arrived full of reassurance. 'I have chosen a particular builder, I have chosen most carefully. This builder, Madame, he will see the workmen turn up and get on with the work, you must not worry, this builder he will take care of it, only not now Madame, not in August, when everyone is on holiday. French people have to take a holiday, no?' He smiled. 'Perhaps Madame did not understand properly when we met?'

Jane shook her head in disbelief. She suspected she would play 'patsy' quite a lot over the coming weeks. At least the smooth talking agent knew how to switch the water on.

There was no point worrying about the delay; she would have to make do with wet wipes and McDonalds for a while longer. While she waited Jane explored the local countryside. She drove past fields full of tall nodding sweet corn, grown as animal fodder in that part of France. She spotted red squirrels, not seen since childhood, running through dense beech wood forests and she marvelled at acres of rushes that grew in low-lying flatlands, although the marshland bordering them seemed perilously close in places.

She drove to the medieval city of Guerande and toured the vast salt marshes beyond—the most northerly salt marshes in Europe where harvesting is still done by hand. Sitting in the car she wound down the window to catch the sharp tang of ozone and the taste of salt on the breeze. She watched suntanned workers open and close a series of wooden sluice gates that allow Atlantic seawater to wash over the network of ponds and salt pans. Salt crystals raked into mounds were bleached by the sun, scoured by the wind and left to dry naturally.

Bypassing the chic seaside resort of La Boule—a bustling, ostentatious place full of luxury boutiques that didn't hold any interest—she kept going to the tiny port of Croisic, perched on the end of the peninsula, where a few fishing boats still operated and the day's catch was auctioned off at the fish market near the jetty. Later she left the beaches of Morbihan behind and drove inland, through the centuries old forest surrounding La Bretesche where she discovered an imposing chateau, built in the early fourteenth century and now a thriving hotel restaurant.

On another foray she drove through La Brière, the brooding marshland that stretched for nineteen thousand hectares from the Vilaine Estuary in the north to Guerande's salt marshes in the west and the Loire Estuary in the South. It formed a vast patchwork of wetlands, rich in marine and birdlife.

People have lived on the edge of the marshland for centuries, digging up peat to burn and using reeds from the water's edge to thatch their houses. She discovered La Briere had the highest concentration of thatched cottages anywhere in France. In Kerhinet, where they had been restored as a tourist attraction, bright red geraniums bloomed on narrow window ledges. Elsewhere the houses had been left to decay. Walls of heavy stone had crumbled and moss grew thick on dark thatched roofs, hinting at cold, damp interiors. The tiny windows let in a mean amount of light and the slow-moving flat marshland was never far away.

Her own house looked luxurious by comparison.

By the end of the first week in September the stonemason and carpenter were on site and Jane lost access to her bedroom. She retreated to the animal shed at the top of the garden. It may have been grubby and full of odd bits of timber and rusting gardening tools, as well as most of the furniture she'd brought from England, but at least it was dry. The sofa, still covered in plastic from the journey over, would do as a bed. She had an emergency loo and she could drive to the local McDonalds for a quick wash and a bite to eat each morning.

Over the next two weeks the stonemason knocked down walls to turn the second bedroom into a kitchen, opening it onto the covered veranda on one side and to the living room on the other. Before long a simple half height wall, with shelving either side, marked the division between the kitchen and the living/dining room. While he was in demolition mode he cut a doorway from the kitchen into the breezeblock annexe with the dirt floor. Jane knew she would have to wait a few years before she could afford to do anything with the annexe, but at least the messy work would be done.

With the stonemason gone for the day she lay on the sofa in the animal shed and looked out across the empty field towards her house. A pair of bats appeared in the gloom, treating her to an acrobatic display, followed by a barn owl that swooped silently across the garden.

Her introduction to life in France was everything she'd hoped it would be. In the heavy silence of that hot summer's night she lay awake, imagining the garden that would gradually take shape and planning the work that needed to be done, listening to the sound of crickets and frogs croaking in the darkness.

7 WATERWORKS

In the weeks after Jane left, I spent my time redecorating her flat—my flat now. I painted the walls white, pulled up the disabled ramp, put doors back on all the cupboards, sanded the floorboards and got rid of the mismatched colour on all the skirting boards.

When I had finished my decorating blitz, several weeks later, I stood back to admire my handiwork. I felt oddly disappointed. The flat seemed cold and empty. Part of its original charm had been Jane, a large part, and I had eliminated all trace of her. I stood in the kitchen, looking out over the back garden that I hadn't managed to tame and decided I would leave it to flourish.

In late September I received the first of a series of letters, each painstakingly hand written by Jane then typed by her good friend Sally and distributed to people eager for news.

September 1993

Well, here is the first epistle from France. Things are progressing as you can see from the fact that I have a telephone. Please don't ring and say that you are coming to stay because I have been evicted until they have got running water on again…I keep going there to see if the plumber has arrived with his JCB but I'm afraid he hasn't…My neighbours on one side have told me to knock on the wall if I need anything in the night (I wonder what the possibilities are!) and the couple opposite are 84 and 82. He rides a bike and grows veg in his garden while she comes over to show me where she had her operation on her knee and tells me about her coronary and has a little weep about the children she has lost. Poor old soul has had a hard life and misses the old lady who used to live in my house. I am also collecting an ever growing group of children, headed by a 16 year old girl who wants to practice her English on me and they all help me with my French. When we have somewhere to sit down, I hope they will play scrabble with me!

With building work halted for the weekend, Jane ventured inside her rubble-strewn house to measure up for curtains. There was a knock at the back door and she looked up to see a woman with short grey hair, who looked to be in her early 50s, standing outside. She was dressed in sturdy shoes, practical work trousers and a cotton shirt. Her striking features carried echoes of great beauty although her weathered expression suggested long days spent outdoors. Jane wheeled across to open the heavy metal door and the younger woman extended her hand.

'Bonjour Madame, Je m'appelle Jeannine Tripon. J'habite à côté.' Her strong voice was warm and clear.

'Ah tray bon!' said Jane, misunderstanding her next-door neighbour's surname. 'Tray bon! Je suis Jane Lambert. Onchantay.' Jane was determined to speak only French. Her comprehension had improved and her vocabulary was growing every day, but her accent still hadn't shifted. Try as she might she still sounded like a BBC announcer from the 1950s reporting on a royal wedding. Faced with someone who clearly hadn't mastered French, Jane's next-door neighbour did the only thing possible. She raised her voice.

'JEANNINE TRIPON.'

Jane smiled as her neighbour looked around the dusty interior, undisguised horror written on her face.

'Mais dis donc, il y a a…IL Y A GRANDE CHOSE A FAIR ICI!'

Jane did her best to explain the plan of works and Jeannine's eyes widened as she stepped over piles of masonry and stacks of timber.

'WHERE ARE YOU SLEEPING?'

Jane pointed to the animal shed at the top of the garden, where her makeshift bed was just visible. Jeannine thrust her head forward.

'Mais que'est ce que c'est que ca? You are sleeping—YOU ARE SLEEPING IN YOUR GARAGE?'

'Just until the workmen have finished. It's not too bad.'

Early the next morning, while Jane was lying in bed, her next-door neighbour trudged up to the top of the garden with a flask of tea and a plate of biscuits. She came back the following day bearing the same thoughtful gift, and each day that Jane slept in her shed, Jeannine arrived with morning tea and biscuits. It was a touching gesture that made Jane feel warmly welcomed and deeply grateful.

Two weeks of sleeping in the animal shed eventually took their toll and Jane was forced to check into the nearest Campanile hotel— a budget hotel chain with good facilities for the disabled. Each day she went back to the house to check on progress. She was itching to move back in. Staying in a hotel—even one as cheap as the local Campanile—had eaten into her budget and she couldn't afford to stay much longer.

Finally, three weeks later, there was a new septic tank in the garden, a semi-functioning bathroom and a kitchen consisting of a microwave, a fridge and a sink. The plumber still had to come back to install the shower and change the height of the sink but at least she had running water and a working loo. It was enough to check out of the hotel and move in.

Autumn brought a cooling breeze from the Atlantic. Lizards scuttled up the garden walls in search of sunshine and damselflies and butterflies fluttered around the pampas grass.

More neighbours gradually approached to introduce themselves. One of the first to emerge was the owner of a house further up the side road, a house that looked even more dilapidated than Jane's. He was a smiling man in his late seventies who spoke grizzled French at great speed, his teeth bared and his mouth stretched into a near permanent grin. Jane was hard pressed to pick up one word in twenty.

She worked out the man's name was Alain Legros, and he was retired from the army where he'd been 'maitre de chiens', which explained why he was happier talking to dogs than to humans. Jane thought he was a brave man to attempt to restore a house in such a rundown condition, especially when she saw how unsteady on his feet he was, but it turned out Alain had no intention of doing anything to his house. He liked it just the way it was, especially the owl that lived in the chimney. Alain was passionate about hunting, growing vegetables and, not surprisingly, dogs. His sausage dog of alarming proportions was a hairy stray called 'Copain'. Jane looked the word up in the dictionary after he'd left, and was delighted to find it meant friend.

Searching for a jumper amongst the bin liners in the shed one afternoon Jane came across an old friend of her own, a treasured teddy bear that had been with her since childhood. She smiled at the ragged bear, held him up to the light and dusted him off, prompting a mouse to run out of his armpit. The tiny mouse darted up Jane's arm, scampered along her neck and disappeared over her shoulder.

Jane's fear of mice is overwhelming—a wild irrational fear, completely disproportionate to the size of the creature—and she let out a piercing scream. Moments later the gate beside the shed swung open and a sombre man in dark canvas trousers and an open neck shirt loomed over her wheelchair, his large hands dwarfed by the size of the cabbage he carried.

'Bonjour Madame, ca va?'

'It was a mouse. Un souris!'

'Ah.'

He silently handed Jane the cabbage. 'Biore. André Biore.'

'Oh. Thank you Monsieur. Jane Lambert.'

André nodded and went on his way. He was one of the many residents of Maca who spoke only if there was something to be said.

The installation of a new septic tank left Jane's garden littered with craters, like a battlefield after the troops have given up and gone home. All the clay from five feet down was brought to the top and dumped there. The only consolation was the arrival of Jean Paul, a dark-haired muscular beauty who came back to fill up the holes, but sadly there was nothing he could do about the clay.

Without concrete paths the garden was a quagmire that worsened in the rain. Thick clumps of heavy mud stuck to Jane's wheels and she dragged it through the house. She made small inroads into the soggy ground by filling in tiny hollows and planting grass and clover but it had little effect against the sea of mud that stretched into the distance. As winter approached and the weather worsened she was forced to give up.

By early November it was clear there was a serious problem with the drains. After a prolonged downpour the local water table rose and prevented water draining from the sinks in the kitchen and the bathroom. Worse still, the septic tank was struggling to cope and the loo wouldn't flush properly. The more it rained the worse it got. The only conclusion Jane could draw was that her house had been built on a flood plain. Maca is on the edge of La Brière, low lying wetlands that contain a wealth of birdlife and plant life, also known as the second largest swamp in France. It was an urgent problem that had to be fixed, and Jane had run out of money.

I heard about the problems and wondered if Jane might give up. Three months into her French adventure the playful heat of summer that buoyed her spirits when she first arrived had been replaced by cold, hard reality. There's nothing romantic about living in a water soaked stone house, without central heating or carpets, in the depths of winter in northern France.

If Jane ever felt down or depressed it happened in winter. Her remedy for depression was a simple concoction of sunshine, warmth, friends and enjoyable activities—all in short supply during the dark winter months in her new home in France. The television had no reception because she couldn't afford to have an aerial fitted—that was a long way down the list of priorities—so she joined the local library and worked her way through an eclectic catalogue of music and film.

Shut indoors on bleak winter evenings, rugged up against the cold, she worked her way through Carmen, Albinoni, Madame Butterfly, Ivor Novello, South Pacific, Carousel, Seven Brides for Seven

Brothers, Gershwin and Ennio Morricone.

In the months after Jane left London I often found myself standing in her old kitchen, fascinated by the wilderness at the back of the flat that teemed with life. London was cold that winter, and weather reports suggested parts of Northern France were also enduring a prolonged cold snap. Night-time temperatures around Nantes regularly dipped well below freezing, colder than it was even in London.

I knew Jane wouldn't be looking forward to Christmas. She once told me that as an only child she hated the forced happiness of it, and things only got worse after her father left. The situation didn't improve much when she grew up either. When Jane was finally released from hospital—and had managed to persuade the authorities that she was capable of looking after her own children—she coped with Christmas by shutting herself in the kitchen with a bottle of sherry. She would emerge triumphant and exhausted several hours later, having produced roast turkey, roast potatoes, vegetables and gravy. Left to her own devices Jane would rather ditch the turkey and trimmings in favour of bread and cheese, with a glass of wine or whisky to wash it down.

The kitchen at Little Ealing Lane was the coldest part of the flat, yet often as I stood at the sink, staring across the garden, I felt an inexplicable brush of warm air against my cheek. Each time it happened, I thought of Jane.

Having promised to stay in touch I picked up the phone in late November and asked how things were going.

'Pas mal, not bad,' Jane said. 'How's the flat?'

'There's something about the heating. Did you ever feel pockets of warm air in the kitchen?

Jane laughed. 'They haven't worked out where I am yet.'

'Who hasn't?'

'The Spirits. Don't worry, they'll find me eventually.'

I realised I missed the company of the exotic woman I'd briefly shared a flat with. On impulse I asked, 'Would you like a visitor before Christmas?' Her response was immediate. 'Oh yes please!' she said. A few days later she rang back. 'I've had an idea,' she said. 'I'm going to throw a party while you're here, to meet the neighbours. Can you bring a few things over?'

'What would you like?

'Mince pies, ginger beer, sausage rolls and chipolata sausages. And trifle.'

8 THE FIRST NOEL

A murky sludge of darkness pressed against the car. There were no streetlights, no cats' eyes and nothing to tell me if we were on the right road. The wiper on the driver's side had stopped working and a dirty film of sleet was smeared across the windscreen, obscuring my vision. The welcome pinpricks of light that drivers follow in the centre of remote English roads—the only thing that prevents them from driving into a ditch—now seemed like the best invention ever.

I had persuaded my good friend Alan, a musician and teacher, to join me for the trip to France. We were driving an old Vauxhall Nova packed with provisions from English supermarkets, and resting on top of the load was Alan's accordion. Never having been to France before he'd thrown himself into the spirit of things and come equipped with what he considered to be an archetypal French musical instrument.

The trip to France had seemed like a great idea when we left London but the drive from St Malo had dispelled our enthusiasm. High winds and heavy rain, now turned to sleet, kept us company all the way and road works had diverted us around Jane's village. We had been forced to approach her house from an unknown direction, and now we felt hopelessly lost.

'We have to turn right somewhere, hers is the house on the corner,' I said, searching in the blackness for clues.

'What number is it?'

'It doesn't have a number. She said we had to turn left at a recycling bin. Is that a recycling bin?'

I squinted at a dark shape in the distance and spotted Jane's car with its distinctive top box, jutting out of a back garden. 'There! This is it!'

We parked, grabbed the bags and braved the sleet, picking our way across the mud towards the back door. Jane's smiling face was visible through the glass, a welcoming beacon of light, and she pushed open the door as we approached.

'Come in, come in! Bonjoor! Whisky anyone? Or would you prefer champagne?'

My image of 'authentic' French interiors was based on magazine features extolling the beauty of dove grey walls, zinc topped tables, oak panelling, puddled curtains, finials, swags, sparkling chandeliers and kitchens full of Le Creuset. I was shocked at how basic Jane's house was. At first glance it had only the bare essentials she would need to survive.

The kitchen consisted of a small bar fridge, a sink, a kettle, a toaster and a microwave on top of the newly built half-height wall that separated the kitchen from the living/dining area. The low wall had open shelves on one side and drawers on the other. The only other furniture in the kitchen was a wooden shelving unit housing pots, pans and the ubiquitous Tupperware.

The chilly bathroom at the back of the house was no different. It had a sink, a loo and a wall-mounted showerhead above a tiled bench. A small electric heater in the tiled bathroom struggled to combat the cold that seeped through a metal-framed, single glazed window.

Jane's love of colour gave the simple house its character. In the bathroom, aquatic green tiles shimmered below walls painted powder blue. The kitchen walls were rich terracotta, the bedroom was blancmange pink and the woodwork was typically French grey-green. Brightly coloured posters of fish, birds, insects, fruit and vegetables—saved from the Guardian newspaper years before—decorated the walls in the kitchen and in the bathroom.

In the dining area mismatched cushions covered the chairs and family photographs lined the shelves. Neat and tidy are two words that could never be used to describe Jane. Very little gets put away, largely because of the effort involved in getting it back out again. Anyway, that's how Jane liked it.

The dining table was covered in a cheery plastic tablecloth and it was home to a growing collection of essentials; correspondence waiting to be dealt with, bottles of wine and water, photographs, boxes of pills, magazines, bowls of nuts and a basket of bread.

A compost bin tucked into the open gap under the sink overflowed with waste and there were piles of paper, cardboard and plastic stacked in the veranda. Jane argued that it wasn't worth driving to the nearest recycling point unless there was enough to fill the boot of the car, so recycling gradually accumulated in available corners.

The main problem was the lack of heating. It was bitterly cold outside—the kind of Dickensian cold that pinches your skin, compresses your skull and makes your bones ache—and not much warmer inside. The stone floors were covered in linoleum and, apart from Jane's bedroom and the new bathroom, the whole of the ground floor was open plan. The wall between the veranda and the kitchen had been knocked through so nothing stopped the bitter cold from seeping through the metal back door and plunging through the plastic corrugated roof, as if it were nothing more substantial than a layer of cling film.

'I might have to put doors between the kitchen and the veranda,' said Jane, as if reading my thoughts. 'It depends how cold it gets.'

I wondered how much colder it *could* get. One of the reasons Jane had wanted to move to France was to escape the brutal British winter. This part of France didn't seem any warmer, and the only heating for the whole of the downstairs area was a portable gas stove.

We huddled around the stove and filled what was left of the evening with champagne, pate, cheese, whisky and talk of Jane's new life in France. Alan kept us entertained with his accordion and at one o'clock in the morning, warmed by food and wine we went to bed. I curled up on a mattress on the floor of Jane's bedroom and Alan slept on a camp bed in the dining room, beneath a noisy control box that rattled its way through the night to provide hot water for the next day.

That night Alan found out more about French plumbing than he ever wanted to know. In the middle of the night he discovered the bathroom flooded and the toilet full. Flushing wasn't an option. The only thing he could find to try and shift the blockage was a misshapen courgette in the compost bin under the sink. After several attempts the impromptu plunger did the trick and Alan rinsed it off, returned it to the compost bin and went back to bed.

The next day a watery sun struggled to break through the low-lying cloud. The field at the back of Jane's house was white with frost and the cold seemed to seep through the walls. It was hard to see the appeal of France on such a bleak day.

'Let's go out,' Jane said, determined to make the most of our visit. We bundled into thick coats, boots, gloves and scarves and drove to the walled city of Guerande, where Handel's Messiah was being performed in the medieval church of St Aubins. Jane parked her car in a side street and we waited while she unloaded her chair and shifted across.

'Want a push?'

'Yes please.'

Our breath billowed in the sub zero temperatures as we trundled across the cobbled street towards the church. If anything it seemed colder inside than it was outside. Jane parked her wheelchair at the end of a pew and I wondered if it was worth it. In spite of her coat, scarf and gloves she looked frozen. What were we doing, sitting in a freezing church when we could have been at home, listening to a recording of Handel's Messiah? I leant across and suggested as much to Jane, who just smiled and tied her scarf around her head.

'Don't worry, it will be worth it,' she said.

Alan nipped out to a café across the square and came back with three plastic cups of hot chocolate and we huddled together, sipping our steaming cups of chocolate, waiting for the performance to start.

As the opening bars of Handel's Messiah filled the church, Jane's face lit up. It was as if the music had found a way straight through to her soul. When the singers joined in the chorus she was transported to a place of beauty that seemed to shut out the cold and I realised then that Jane would have put up with any amount of discomfort to access that kind of beauty.

I helped prepare dinner when we got back while Alan wandered through the village, taking photographs before the light faded.

'Jane, are you glad you've made the move?'

'Yes.'

'In spite of the cold, the damp, the flooding and all the work that needs to be done?'

Jane smiled and nodded. 'This is exactly where I want to be. I spent 20 years living in that flat on Little Ealing Lane, and I never once slept through the night. I've got the ears of a bat. If it wasn't buses or cars it was planes, or drunks on the way home from the pub, or the milkman at four o'clock in the morning.'

She laughed. 'For the first time in years I can sleep through the night. There's no traffic to wake me up and no mortgage to pay. I know there's a lot of work to be done, but I'll get there.'

Dinner that night was courgette bake. Alan stared in horror at the steaming vegetables as Jane brought the dish to the table and he hurriedly pushed back his chair.

'Excuse me, I just...'

'Are you alright?'

'No...Yes...I just need to check on something.'

He darted into the kitchen, stuck his head under the sink to check the compost bin and came back to the table looking relieved.

The following day we decorated the house with strings of paper chains in preparation for the party. Earlier in the week Jane had made up a simple invitation, inviting guests to attend at half past six for 'les aperitifs', and she had hand delivered invitations to all the inhabitants of Maca.

The 'spread' on the dining table was Jane's way of introducing her neighbours to English food. It consisted of toasted crumpets, cheddar cheese and pineapple on sticks, chipolata sausages, mince pies, trifle and a Christmas cake Jane had made in the microwave. Worried it might not be as succulent as a boiled fruitcake she had liberally spiked it with brandy. The smell of alcohol seeped through the thick white icing.

One by one, punctual to the minute, guests filed through the door. It was obvious that this wasn't a young village. Most of the guests were in their sixties, seventies or eighties. Wary-looking men in dark overcoats, thick trousers and heavy boots sat on one side of the room and women in pleated skirts and dark slacks sat opposite. When the chairs ran out they took up standing positions along the same divide.

Jane's immediate next-door neighbour, Jeannine, arrived with her husband Robert, a thick set, solid man with a square head, eyes partially hidden under bushy eyebrows and a mane of black hair that looked borrowed from someone younger. His dour expression vanished when he smiled.

Former owners Monsieur and Madame Lagueux were also there. After they'd sold the house to Jane—a house Madame Lagueux's mother had also lived in—they hadn't gone far, moving just a few doors down. There was Lucien, a smiling parody of a handsome Frenchman in his early seventies, tight dungarees straining over his ample stomach. He was short and stout, with a body as solid as a turnip, and close cropped grey hair that topped an open, smiling face. Therese, his wife, was an unexpectedly chic woman with short grey-blonde hair, glasses and a great sense of humour.

Jean Yves, their son, was a slight man in his early fifties, who worked in the laboratory at the nearby oil refinery and lived in a house directly opposite his parents. He was equally good looking, with black hair, a wiry frame and eyes that looked on the world with quiet amusement. His wife, Francoise, was a slender French beauty with short dark hair and a serious face, boundless energy bubbling under the manicured surface of her neatly pressed jeans and tailored white shirt.

None of Jane's immediate neighbours had ever been to England and few, if any, had ever had any dealings with someone from England, certainly not an eccentric woman in a wheelchair. They were typically, and traditionally, French. Many had been born in Maca, they'd grown up in Maca and they'd lived in Maca all their lives.

I wondered what they made of Jane. Even in this remote spot they must have heard stories of English people buying holiday homes in France. How long did they give her? A month? Two months? They must have thought she would head back to the UK come winter. She was English after all. This would surely be a holiday home, that's what the English did. It was an odd place to buy a holiday home, but that's the English for you. They wouldn't have expected her to live here on her own, not a woman in a wheelchair without any family. And yet here she was in early December, with Christmas fast approaching, showing no signs of leaving.

I handed around plates of mince pies and sausage rolls, Alan offered drinks and Jane made conversation, with limited success. None of the guests spoke English and although Jane's French had improved in the short time she'd been there, she still couldn't master the accent. Because of that, people assumed she couldn't understand more than a few words of French. Alan spoke no French at all and mine was definitely rusty.

'Ca va?' I said brightly to an elderly man in the corner.

'Oui. Ca va.'

It was hard going but the guests didn't seem to mind. The atmosphere was convivial enough and no one was in any hurry to leave. They were curious about the new resident of Maca. The women chatted amongst themselves and Alan, Jane and I kept handing out food and drink.

The success of the night was a box of crackers, unheard of in France, which transformed the dour and formal guests into excitable children, screeching at the sound of the crackers and gamely putting on their party hats.

'If you need anything, ANYTHING AT ALL, YOU MUST KNOCK ON THE WALL, d'accord?' said Jeannine, sporting the bright orange crown of a perky hen. She smiled at me and nodded. Perhaps she thought I was a relation of Jane's.

'Que'est ce qu'elle fait ici?' The old man who posed the question stared at me as I offered him a plate of cubed cheese and tinned pineapple on sticks. I struggled to find an answer. What *was* Jane doing there? It was an unusual move by anyone's standards. Jane liked to joke that people probably thought she was an alcoholic, drawn to France by the prospect of cheap booze, but I knew that wasn't it. Jane was drawn by the prospect of creating a new life for herself, the chance to do things her own way without anyone controlling her. I decided to say, she's looking for an adventure, and when I couldn't think of the French word for adventure I took a guess.

'Elle cherche une aventure,' I said.

The old man nodded and took a sip of pastis. He narrowed his eyes and looked across at Jane, seeming to weigh her up. I could guess what he was thinking. It must have been difficult for a traditional French family man of his age to understand why someone like Jane, disabled or not, would make such a move. Why retire to France, where she had no family and knew no one? Later that night I discovered that probably wasn't what he was thinking at all.

When all the guests had left I checked in the dictionary to find what the word aventure normally means in French. *Aventure: a fling; an affair; a sexual liaison.* I told Jane's neighbours she had come to France looking to have an affair. Jane thought it was a great joke that I'd given her such a racy reputation. As it turned out, I wasn't far wrong.

Alan and I drove back to England and Jane's good friend, Pam, flew out to stay that first Christmas. Her impressions of the house weren't much changed by the work Jane had done. Pam still thought the house was a dump. The reality of staying in the depths of winter wasn't pleasant. A biting Atlantic wind battered the windows, rattled the crumbling veranda, struck the metal back door and fingered its way through every gap under the sills and every chink in the frames. The ancient electric control box that regulated the hot water system, which was mounted on the wall above the sofa, rattled its way through the night directly above where Pam was trying to sleep. In desperation she took her bedding into the bathroom, put a blanket on the floor and tried to sleep with her head jammed against the pedestal of the toilet.

Jane did her best to keep Pam entertained to make up for the less than comfortable accommodation. Wintry days were spent driving around. They visited the medieval city of Guerande, the town of Croisic and the ruins of an ancient chateau in Herbignac. They visited Arboug, St Lyphard and St Andre des Eaux. In the end though, no amount of sightseeing could compensate for the draughty, unheated house with a hole in the roof. Nothing could disguise the leaking veranda covered in corrugated plastic, drains that backed up when it rained and a quagmire of a back garden.

Defeated by the discomfort, Pam cut her trip short and Jane drove her friend to the airport in Nantes. Pam caught the next flight back to London and Jane drove back to Maca alone. The rain didn't stop falling all day.

At midday on New Year's Eve Jane pulled on woollen socks, thick trousers, a second jumper, scarf and coat for the short drive to Donges. The blanket of cold hadn't lifted for days. Mist crept in from the marshes that lay unseen at the edge of Maca and it seeped across the hushed streets, draping a heavy cloak of silence over all it touched.

There were few people around on the short drive into Donges and the town square was practically deserted. Jane parked her car and lowered the wheelchair from its overhead box, the cold cutting through her layers of clothing as she shifted across from the car. She blew on her stiffened fingers before slotting the metal footplates and armrests into place. She was heading for the bank, the supermarket and the library.

With Pam gone Jane wanted an uplifting album to listen to, or a decent film to watch. Her neighbours would be feasting with friends and family that night and she wanted something to occupy her time. When darkness fell, the evenings dragged. She still didn't have access to French television so she existed on a diet of whatever films and music she could borrow from the local library. The radio was all well and good for practising French but the strain of trying to catch what was said was too much for her. Tonight she wanted to relax.

That crisp sunny day in February when Jane had seen her house for the first time had been a fluke. This was the norm: mist rolling in from the sea, hovering over low-lying wetlands, settling on the countryside and smothering it. The area she had chosen to live was notoriously foggy and damp in winter, just the kind of weather she hated. She'd made it through the first six months, what about the next six? There were two or three months of bleak weather ahead, and without proper heating it was as much as she could do to keep warm.

She bought the few things she needed from the near empty supermarket, gave up on the bank when she saw it was closed and pushed her chair across the frost whitened pavements to the library. There was a cheerful notice pinned to the front door.

Ferme. Bonne année!

And a Happy New Year to you too, she sighed. She turned around, headed back to the car and drove home. Lights were coming on in neighbouring houses as she drove into the village and the smell of wood smoke hung in the air. There was a tantalising whiff of onion soup and roast garlic as she manoeuvred out of the car and she caught a glimpse of a figure hurrying past, wrapped up against the cold. He had a scarf tucked neatly under his chin and a bottle of red wine clutched under his arm.

'Bonne année!' He called.

'Bonne année!' Jane replied.

She rested one shopping bag on her lap and tucked the other on the footrest between her then she scrunched across the frozen mud towards the back door, fumbling in her bag for the keys. Her fingers registered a sting of cold as they brushed against the metal doorframe and she hurriedly pushed inside. That morning's washing up lay in the sink and, until water levels subsided, that's where it would have to stay. She checked the bathroom to find water lapping at the edge of the toilet seat. It was a dispiriting sight.

That night Jane pulled on another jumper, poured herself a whisky and wrote out a list of resolutions—fix the drains, the septic tank and the heating; start the loft, the new roof, the solar panel and the cement paths; paint the outside; plant trees and climbers; speak better French.

It was an ambitious list.

9 WET BLANKET

Jane went to bed early on New Year's Eve, slept badly and woke to the sound of rain drumming on the corrugated plastic roof of the veranda. The weather forecast promised more. She lingered in bed, reluctant to face the prospect of a sink full of dirty dishes and a pile of dirty washing that couldn't be tackled until the water levels dropped.

As midday approached she forced herself to leave the comfort of her warm nest and she got dressed quickly. Washing could wait. In the living room she put on a Nana Mouskouri album, picked up a pack of playing cards and lay the first card face up on the table. She took her time, turning the cards over one by one, searching for patterns and sequences as the individual lines of cards gradually spread across the table in front of her. The game of patience helped her unwind, easing the tension in her shoulders. It was a gentle reminder that building a new life in France would take time. Time was something Jane had plenty of.

A knock at the back door interrupted the game and Jane looked up to see a shivering Jeannine and Robert, her immediate next-door neighbours, smiling through the glass. She put down the cards and wheeled across to open the door.

'Bonjour Jeanne! BONNE ANNEE!' Jeannine scrutinised Jane's face for signs of comprehension and Jane obliged with a greeting of her own.

'Bonne année! Entrez, entrez.'

Jeannine gave a broad smile.

'ALORS, CA VA?'

Jane smiled, nodded and reached for a bottle.

'Apereteef?'

Jane's understanding of French was well advanced by now and her spoken French had improved too, it was only the accent that defeated her. She'd studied choral work and she had a good singing voice, so if what people said about having a 'good ear' was true it should have been easy. As it was, no matter how hard she tried, when Jane spoke French it sounded like she was speaking the perfect clipped English of a member of the British Raj. She poured her guests a drink and listened to Jeannine fret.

'In the middle of the night—IN THE MIDDLE OF THE NIGHT—remember, you must bang on the wall—BANG ON THE WALL, YES?' Jeannine thumped the party wall to make sure Jane understood. 'ANYTHING YOU NEED, YOU UNDERSTAND?'

Jane nodded. She doubted if the kind of thing she might want in the middle of the night was the kind of thing Jeannine had in mind, but it was sweet of her all the same. Jeannine had developed an almost parental concern for her and Jane knew she was fortunate to have found such welcoming, considerate neighbours. Another knock at the door announced the arrival of Lucien and Therese, Lucien with his bright eyes, knowing smile and trademark overalls and Therese as elegant, good humoured and quietly spoken as always.

'Bonne année Jeanne!'

'Bonne année!'

Lucien sipped his aperitif and looked around the house, his dark eyes sliding into corners, taking in the improvements Jane had made.

'Jeanne, your house is famous, did you know?'

'Really? How?'

'La Résistance, they used to meet here during the war.'

Jane wondered if she'd understood him properly. Lucien inclined his head. 'You have a side annexe, yes?'

'Yes, that's right.'

Lucien, with his innocent appearance and knowing eyes, nodded slowly and Jane wondered if he might have been involved. 'Were you a member of the Resistance?' she asked. Lucien held a finger to the side of his nose and smiled, untold secrets shimmering in his eyes like sparkling nuggets of black gold. More aperitifs were poured and Jane relaxed in the easy rhythm of conversation between people who have known each other for decades. She let it wash over her and tried to pick up what she could.

Francoise called in later that afternoon and found Jane still listening to the Nana Mouskouri album. She stopped to listen, her head tilted to one side like a blackbird.

'I like that,' she said.

'Do you? I'll make you a copy.'

Jane was eager to repay the many acts of kindness she'd been shown. Life could have been very different if the village hadn't welcomed her into the community.

While they waited for the tape to finish, the energetic Francoise glanced at the washing up in the sink. She hadn't missed the pile of dirty washing lying on the floor by the machine either. 'Jeanne, can I help you with something? Perhaps the washing up?'

Jane smiled and explained the problem with the water levels. She shrugged off the inconvenience. 'It won't last long. Once it stops raining, the water will be gone. I hope!'

Francoise wasn't convinced. She was always ready to step in when there was a problem to be solved.

'Mais non. You cannot wait. I will take your washing and I will put it through my machine, c'est simple.'

The residents of Maca formed a close-knit community, and any concerns they might have had about Jane being in a wheelchair were dispelled early on. Far from worrying that they might be called on to look after a disabled woman who had suddenly appeared in their midst, they now worried that Jane was too independent for her own good. Jane was willing to put up with a level of discomfort others would have baulked at, and she was also fiercely independent and more than capable of looking after herself.

Whilst they admired her tenacity and independence, Jane's neighbours were determined to offer the help they thought she needed. Of course, that wasn't always the help Jane wanted.

Suffering an upset stomach after Christmas celebrations of rich French food and wine, all of which had to be sampled, Jane consulted a naturopath. She was given a regime of different tablets and powders, each to be taken in certain doses at various times of the day.

She painstakingly opened each box, slid out the contents, slit open the blister pockets, wrote the dose on the edge of each packet and positioned the opened packets on a shelf within easy reach. The next time she looked, someone had thoughtfully closed all the packets, stacked them in a neat pile and placed them at the back of the shelf, just out of reach.

Winter dragged on and every type of bleak weather blanketed the region. Frost, fog, sleet, hail, storms, wind and rain tested Jane's resolve. The weather trapped her indoors so she invited people over. Lucien and Therese and Francoise and Jean Yves called in with their children, Charlotte and Benjamin, to share Christmas cake and drinks. Monseiur and Madame Lagueux came with chocolates and Jane gave them a bowl of hyacinth bulbs in return. More neighbours called in, more chocolates and more hyacinths were dispensed and still the cold wind battered the house.

Jane's only source of heat in the open plan kitchen, dining and living area was her small portable gas fire. Realising that Jane would struggle to change a heavy gas bottle Lucien had appointed himself her official gasman.

'Please call me when the gas runs out,' he said. 'I will change the bottle.'

Jane took Lucien at his word and every couple of weeks she rang him. She didn't like to bother him at night, so if the gas ran out in the evening she would wrap herself in a blanket and go to bed early. The only other source of heat was a small electric fan heater in the bathroom, which did little to dispel the bone-chilling cold that seeped through the walls and rose up from the tiled floor.

The problem was made worse by wide gaps around the doors and windows that gave the wind free run of the house. Draughts fingered their way into every corner and the worst place was the kitchen, where cold crept in like a burglar prowling through an unlocked house. In the end Jane had to use some of the money she'd set aside for repairing the roof on a new set of double doors, which were installed between the kitchen and the veranda to keep the worst of the weather at bay.

In mid January, just when it seemed winter would never end, the camellia tree at the front of the house burst into flower. It heralded a spate of sunny days and a bright new moon that lit up the garden at night. Crocus blooms, shining yellow through the gloom, brought the first hint of winter's demise at the end of January and the jonquil Jane planted in autumn rewarded her with fat buds, holding out the promise of early flowers and rich fragrance. Even the first dandelion, unfurling its spiky flower head, was a welcome sight.

Jane took cuttings of daphne and mimosa and wrote an upbeat letter to friends.

January 1994

Happy New Year to you all, or as we say in France, Bonne Année a tous....I enjoyed all your Christmas cards and so have my friends. They don't go in for them a lot here and mine hanging round my living room have caused great interest. Thank you all so much and it's lovely to hear your news.

In reality, she was worried about money. The old Metro she'd driven over from England had broken down and was in the garage, awaiting urgent repairs. She'd broken a front tooth and needed emergency dental work and the plumber still hadn't sent in his bill. What had arrived was the estimate for the new roof, which was more than she'd expected. She was also forced to admit that the most effective way of making the house warmer would be to replace the veranda. The cost of doing that would be substantial.

For all Jane's make do and mend attitude—a plant trough used for video storage, the legs cut off an old shelf unit to make it a suitable height, old trousers cut up to make cushion covers—money was flowing out and not much was coming in. The odd English lesson was never going to be enough to supplement her pension and pay for essential repairs to the house. There were land taxes, TVA taxes, stamp duties, residential taxes—the list went on. As the weeks slipped by and money kept flowing out Jane decided to apply for a loan.

The bank manager at the local branch of Credit Agricole quizzed her on income, expenditure, pension payments and budgets, nodding his head as Jane ran through the figures. He frowned and the corners of his mouth drooped towards his chin as he listened attentively to what Jane was saying. Eventually he shook his head, reluctant to pass on bad news.

'It is possible,' he said. 'Maybe. But I must be honest with you Madame Lambert it will not be easy. Perhaps you would come and see me next week and bring your local tax papers.'

Hedging her bets, Jane called at Le Tabac on the way home and bought a lottery ticket, just in case.

That night she sat in the dining room, listening to a fearsome west wind that shook the plastic veranda roof while heavy rain splashed into puddles of mud outside the back door. As the water level rose in the kitchen sink, her anxiety rose with it.

After dinner she tied a belt around her chest to stop the pain of indigestion, scoffed a bar of chocolate followed by a gin and tonic and wrote a note to herself on her calendar.

Will I ever meet these expenses? Stop panicking. There is sufficient money, even if the loan doesn't come through. JUST STOP SPENDING.

The next day she opened the back door and wheeled outside. A pair of green and yellow great tits swooped across the mud and the air smelt of damp, rich earth. She caught a fleeting glimpse of a woodpecker as the watery sun pushed its way through the clouds. Then she heard the sound of a turtledove to the north.

Winter seemed to be retreating in front of her eyes. A bumblebee landed on the windowsill and a Red Admiral fluttered through the flourishing dandelion heads. The sight of a brimstone yellow butterfly confirmed it; spring had finally arrived. She had survived her first winter in France. She celebrated with oysters and salad for lunch, washed down with a bottle of Macon, and spent the next two days in bed with an upset stomach.

I marvelled at Jane's ability to cling so steadfastly to her dream, admired her absolute refusal to be overwhelmed by the task ahead and wondered if life in Maca would force her to become more conservative. Jane had moved to a traditional French village where all the usual trappings of modern life were absent; there was no mains gas supply, no mains sewage, no satellite dishes and no internet.

If Jane asked Alain what his plans for the weekend were, he would grin and say, 'I will be shooting rabbit.' His eyes would darken with anticipation as he stared into the distance. 'Or maybe wild boar.'

Widows wore black and married women were hardly more adventurous, sporting knee length skirts in navy, grey or dark green. Thick woollen slacks in winter and dark grey coats were all the rage.

Jane hated black and she refused to wear it. Her trademark outfits were buttercup yellow trousers teamed with a pink t-shirt and a flowing cardigan in splashes of purple, aqua, white and magenta, or a checked shirt in yellow, pink, lilac and lime green worn with a spotted hat in orange and ivy. Purple, mauve, cerise, turquoise, red, amber, violet, aubergine, scarlet—preferably all worn at the same time—were all Jane would ever consider.

Far from becoming more conservative Jane took the opposite approach. With the advent of spring she decided to change her hair colour.

The pharmacy in Donges was a gleaming emporium of anti-ageing creams, cellulite treatments and homeopathic remedies. There were specialist shampoos, crystal bottles of designer fragrance and a bewildering array of hair dyes. Jane wheeled towards an assistant, whose slender body was encased in a tight-fitting white coat.

The assistant exuded the supreme self-confidence of a catwalk model. Her hair was cut in a sleek bob, her make-up applied with precision and she was doused in expensive perfume. Her image was reflected multiple times in a series of mirrors behind the glass shelves, and her poise would have made most customers wish they'd checked the mirror before they left home. Not Jane. She wheeled up to the counter, lifted her head and smiled, shooting a beam of light from her baby blue eyes.

'Bonjoor!'

The assistant afforded Jane a brief glimpse of perfectly white teeth. 'Bonjour Madame. May I help you?'

'I'd like to change my hair colour.'

The assistant stared at Jane's hair, already dyed a deep chestnut brown, and smiled indulgently. 'Perhaps, Madame, you would like to go a little lighter?'

'No thank you, I'd like something more adventurous. I'd like something brighter.'

The shop assistant hesitated. 'Brighter, Madame? But your hair is already very bright.'

Jane held up a packet. 'What about this one?' The woman on the packet sported a mass of flame coloured hair, like a tropical sunset or a raging bushfire. It was the tequila sunrise of hair dyes.

'That one Madame?'

'Yes.'

The assistant faltered. 'But Madame...' Her body trembled under the tight-fitting white coat. 'It...it is orange Madame!'

'Yes, it's lovely isn't it? I'll take it.'

Armed with the packet of dye, Jane went home and shut herself in the bathroom. An hour later she emerged, triumphant. The bathroom was awash with soapy water, the towels were streaked with dye and Jane had bright orange hair.

She rummaged through a pile of clothes in the bedroom, held up a silky green jumper to her face and smiled at the contrast. It was like having a brand new wardrobe. Blouses, trousers, scarves, earrings, necklaces and hats all took on striking new tones when held against her hair. She looked like an exotic bulb, flowering unexpectedly in the gloom of a dim forest. Added to her bright red wheelchair, Jane was hard to miss.

In spite of the eccentric clothes and the bright orange hair, Jane was readily accepted as part of the community. She'd earned the respect of locals by consistently speaking French, no matter how imperfect it may have been at the start, and she had stuck it out through the long winter. It was obvious to everyone that Jane hadn't bought the house as a holiday cottage. She was there for the long haul.

10 DIG DEEP

More neighbours emerged to meet the colourful new resident of Maca. Marie Desbois, an 80-year-old widow prone to tears, called in for a cup of tea bearing two small cakes tucked into the pocket of her apron. Her purpose was to have a good cry. It didn't matter that Jane couldn't follow half of what was said, Marie needed a sympathetic friend who would listen to her troubles.

There was sixteen-year-old Charlotte, an attractive girl with clear skin and shoulder length brown hair, daughter of Francoise and Jean Yves and granddaughter of Lucien and Therese. Charlotte spoke a little English and offered to act as Jane's interpreter. She was captivated by the exotic Englishwoman who had arrived so unexpectedly in Maca, especially when Jane died her hair bright orange.

Several people came for English lessons including Eric, a diligent young student who studied hard and progressed quickly, hampered only by his mother who insisted on 'helping' around the house during Eric's lesson. The help was more of a hindrance and Jane discouraged it, knowing his mum's presence made concentration more difficult for the teenager. Christine Biore—wife of the laconic cabbage bearing Andre—turned up with her daughter, ten year old Angelique, to request English lessons in return for cleaning duties. Not many of Jane's pupils could afford to pay for lessons so she gladly accepted help around the house in return.

No one in the village was particularly well off but what they had, they shared. Jeannine and Robert kept a brood of laying hens in their back garden and they were also rearing a pig. An orphaned lamb promised more delights to come. The year before it was goat, the year before that, chickens.

Each week Lucien walked his handful of sheep through the village and let them graze at the back of a house opposite Jane's, where the owner was too old and frail to cut the grass.

When Jeannine and Robert slaughtered the pig they'd been rearing everyone benefited. An excited Jeannine knocked at Jane's back door one morning, waving a bloody parcel in the air. 'PORK CHOPS! SAUCISSONS!'

Therese called in one afternoon with a gift of pate and she went away with a bottle of home-made ginger beer. Eggs, rabbit pie or chicken casserole were all produced from what was grown or raised in neighbouring back gardens, and Jane often found herself the recipient of her neighbours' generosity. She responded with bottles of ginger beer, cups of tea, cakes and biscuits.

Jane rarely asked for help but she discovered her new neighbours didn't wait to be asked. When her car wouldn't start, Lucien popped over to fix it. When she found it hard to stomach the rich food she'd been sampling and stomach cramps kept her in bed, Monique called in with a foul-tasting potion from the chemist and Charlotte called in with peppermints. She told her mum, who told Therese, and they all dropped by to see what they could do to help.

One morning Jane tumbled out of her chair when she was getting dressed. It wasn't unusual, she often slipped out of her chair when she was getting into the car, getting out of bed, washing, cleaning or simply reaching for something too far away, but on this particular day she somehow ended up wedged between the bed and the wall, blocking the door into the bedroom. It was several hours before Jeannine discovered her and, when she did, the only way in was through the bedroom window.

'Jeanne, you must have a panic button,' said Jeannine as she clambered over the windowsill, brushing away a cobweb.

'Why?'

'What if you fall again?'

'Then I'll stay where I am until someone finds me. They will eventually.'

'Tetu! Do you hear me?'

Jeannine was right; Jane was stubborn. It was a stubbornness born from a determination to maintain her independence at all costs, and if that meant falling out of her chair and having to wait several hours for help, so be it. Her only concession was to tie a belt around her chair when she went out, or loop the strap of her handbag over the arms of the wheelchair.

For all the friendship her neighbours offered, and their generous warmth of welcome, Jane missed friends and family more than she liked to admit. The move to France had given her the chance to create a new life for herself but she'd taken on a huge task. There were times when even Jane, with all her optimism, wasn't sure she was up to it.

The bank loan was turned down and the lottery ticket didn't win, but Jane was determined to focus on the positive. The smallest green shoots gave her hope and the briefest glimpse of a wildflower at the side of the road lifted her spirits. The reality though, was that her own back garden was a near-empty, boggy field, comprised largely of clay and punctuated by a few young plants that would take years to mature.

Jane dragged herself away from looming depression by counting her blessings. She looked for beauty and became a master in the art of seeing it. Instead of focussing on the oil refinery when she drove to the supermarket she stared at ditches at the side of the road. It didn't help her driving but she found beauty in abundance.

In early spring she spotted wild orchids, dog daisies and red clover. Batchelor's Button—another name for the cornflowers that used to grow wild in England until intensified farming and excessive use of herbicides turned it into an endangered species—flourished at the base of hedgerows. She spotted Cuckoo Pint, its purple spotted leaves heralding the arrival of tall swaying flower spikes and in late spring she found Ragged Robin and White Campion, all flourishing at the side of the road.

Her fledgling back garden was less successful. On wet days (and there were plenty of those) the garden turned into a claggy swamp. If she wanted to plant anything she had to first struggle through mud. Her wheels sank into it. It clung to her tyres, coated her footplates, caked her shoes and oozed and squelched its way through the spokes on her wheels. Mud stuck to everything she touched—wheels, hands, clothes, furniture and floors—and after a session in the garden it was difficult to move for the weight of clay and mud that clung to her. She trailed it through the house like a giant slug. It was a problem that had to be fixed, and Jane had an idea how to fix it.

The old-fashioned doorbell tinkled as Jane pushed her way into the wheelchair shop in St Nazaire. The young assistant looked up, smiling at the sight of the colourful figure in a red wheelchair slowly making her way towards the counter, orange hair peeking out of a green hat, purple jumper billowing above yellow trousers.

'Bonjour Madame.'

'Bonjoor Madamoiselle. Do you have big wheels?'

'Big wheels Madame?'

'Yes, like on a mountain bike.'

The assistant raised her eyebrows. 'A mountain bike? I'm afraid not Madame. This is a shop for disabled people.'

Jane shifted in her chair and suppressed a smile. 'Yes I thought it might be,' she said.

The assistant waited to see if there was anything else she could help with. 'I have a problem,' Jane continued. 'I keep getting my wheels stuck in mud. Can you suggest anything?'

The assistant considered for a moment. 'Perhaps you should keep out of the mud, Madame?' Jane nodded and the assistant smiled, warming to her task. 'You could spray your wheels with oil, Madame?'

Jane had visions of an oil slick joining the mud she'd already spread across the kitchen floor. She pictured herself sliding into a corner, helplessly trapped until someone had the foresight to sprinkle vinegar onto the mix.

With a sigh she backed her chair towards the door. 'Yes, thank you, most helpful. Merci!' She drove home and stared at the quagmire. The solution was obvious. She needed a concrete path.

One windy day in late May, Jane tied a belt around her waist, looped it over the back of her chair and wheeled out to the garden. The heavy downpour that had drenched the garden earlier that morning was just what she needed—it left the ground soft enough to dig.

She fought her way across the mud to the old animal shed, dragged a wheelbarrow out of the dusty interior and pushed it over the uneven ground towards the back door. When the wheelbarrow was in position she leant forward, stabbed a trowel into the deep clay at her feet and eased a small clod away. Leaning on the arm of the wheelchair for support she sat up, tossed the lump of clay into the wheelbarrow and heard it hit the bottom with a satisfying wet thud.

Jane had decided she would dig for as long as it took to create a channel. One day, a concrete path would be poured there, or maybe she'd put down pavers. She reckoned it would take about two years to dig a channel from one end of the garden to the other. She bent back down to her task.

She'd been working steadily for about an hour when her next-door neighbour, Robert, walked past. He lifted his hat.

'Bonjour Jeanne, ca va?'

Jane waved her trowel. 'Ca va merci Robert.'

Robert stopped and looked more closely at what she was doing. 'Jeanne, what are you going to do with all that mud?' he asked, pointing at the wheelbarrow.

Jane smiled. 'I'm hoping someone will wheel it over to that patch of ground in the corner and empty it,' she said. Robert obliged and Jane revised her estimate. Maybe 18 months.

After a long day of digging Jane gave up just as dusk fell. She looked up to see a new moon lying on its back, and Venus, bright near the setting sun. Small clumps of young plants were silhouetted against the gathering dark but they struggled to break the monotony of the empty field. The muddy track that led nowhere would need months of digging before any concrete could be laid. The chill wind made her jaw throb, aggravating a toothache that had started earlier that afternoon, so she retreated inside for a hot shower to warm herself up.

She undressed quickly, shivering as the cold fingered its way under the bathroom door and seeped across the tiled floor. Shifting from her chair to the wooden seat, she pushed her wheelchair aside then switched on the shower. The tension in her muscles eased as hot water flowed across her goose pimpled skin and she put her head down to shampoo her hair, watching the soapy water flow towards the drain.

Instead of disappearing down the drain, the water surged past. By the time Jane had rinsed the shampoo from her hair, floodwater had swept across the bathroom floor and seeped under the door. She towelled dry, got dressed and splashed her wheelchair through the flood in search of a mop and bucket. Cursing the plumber, she dragged the bucket back into the bathroom and mopped up as best she could then she shut the door and pushed cardboard underneath to soak up the excess. A sodden pile of sheets lay on the floor outside the bathroom, waiting to go into the machine. Let them wait, she thought. She sank a whisky to ease the nagging pain in her tooth and went to bed.

All night long foul water bubbled up from the drain in the bathroom and seeped under the door, threatening to invade the rest of the house. A mass of soggy cardboard pushed into the gap under the door was all that separated Jane from the encroaching flood. She lay awake, listening to rain pummel the corrugated plastic roof on the veranda and tried to keep visions of raw sewage out of her head.

Next morning there was a mess of congealed cardboard wedged under the bathroom door and the unmistakable smell of blocked drains. She took the calendar off the wall and scribbled an uncharacteristically gloomy response. 'I'm depressed,' she wrote.

Jeannine called in for morning tea and spotted the messy cardboard pushed under the bathroom door. Jane explained about the previous night's flood, doing her best to make light of the problem but Jeannine wasn't fooled for a moment. 'Ah non! ENCORE?' She swung into action, took a bowl of dirty dishes back to her house and alerted Francoise, who collected the soggy sheets.

When Francoise brought the freshly laundered sheets back later that night she was accompanied by her husband, Jean Yves. All three gathered in the bathroom as rain drummed on the corrugated plastic roof. The foul smell had intensified and water filled the bowl of the toilet. They watched it lap at the edge of the rim. Jean Yves scratched the dark stubble on his chin; his normally cheerful expression replaced by grim suspicion.

'Do you have a plunger?' he asked.

Jane rummaged in the kitchen and came back with a bent coat hanger. 'Will this do?' She handed Jean Yves the piece of wire and he waggled it into the drain, causing a putrid smell to drift upwards. An ominous gurgle sounded deep in the toilet and Jean Yves took a step back. 'That doesn't sound good,' he said, narrowing his eyes.

'What?'

'That noise. It sounds like your shower and your toilet are connected. That is a big problem. Perhaps there is also a problem with your septic tank.' He shook his head and Jane wondered what else could go wrong.

'Is there a solution?' she asked.

Jean Yves cheered up. 'But of course Jeanne. There is always a solution. You have only to ask the plumber to come back.'

All week Jane mopped and cleaned, pushing contaminated floodwater back down the drain that came up as fast as she cleared it. The foul smell seeped through the entire house—so much for the romance of living in France. To add to the plumbing problem, Jane leant forward with the mop one morning and stretched a little too far. She slipped out of her chair, adding severe bruising to her aching muscles.

The plumber distanced himself from the problem. 'I am sorry Madame Lambert, I have done as much as I can. Maybe if you plant some trees? They will help the soak-away system.'

'The 'soak-away' system?'

'Ah yes, that is most important Madame Lambert.' Jane suspected the 'soak-away' system was a peculiarly French approach to plumbing, possibly unique to her plumber.

I heard about Jane's problems with plumbing—filtered through her ever-optimistic prism—and I wondered if she might give up. She had survived winter in a largely unheated, uncarpeted house in northern France. That alone would have been bad enough, without the threat of raw sewage seeping up through the drains.

I knew the house in France was a means to an end, a way for Jane to gain her independence and freedom, and as such she was prepared to accept a level of discomfort few others would tolerate, but surely there was a limit? Her frugal approach was necessary and admirable, but it didn't do much to improve her comfort.

In the days when whole economies were built on credit, Jane took a different approach. If she couldn't afford it, she didn't buy it. A sheet of plastic tacked across the window was her affordable answer to double-glazing. She accepted the haphazard way the house was developing, and the on-going problems with drainage, as a necessary part of the process. One day, the French house would become a comfortable home but that day was a long way off. Others might have fled the scene, but not Jane. She'd lived in worse places.

When Jane came out of hospital she was housed in a pre-fabricated house, one of thousands that were conceived in 1944 as a temporary measure to solve the UK's housing crisis. Cities such as London, Liverpool and Bristol had been extensively bombed and vast swathes of housing stock were destroyed. Prefabs, as they were known, were the affordable answer.

Built using scrap metal from wartime salvage, recycled aluminium and asbestos (in those days considered a safe building material), each prefab was an exact copy of its neighbour. They were flimsy, single storey oblongs, with windows either side of a central front door. Hundreds were constructed on dozens of small estates and they were kitted out with modern conveniences. Everyone acknowledged they weren't any good at keeping the heat in, or the cold out, but since they were only a short-term solution, no one cared. They were expected to last ten years at most.

Jane was sent to live in hers when she came out of hospital in 1958, when it was already 14 years old. Her youngest son, Roger, born when she was paralysed by polio, was five years old, and like all her children he'd been taken into care. Over the next few years Jane fought to get the children back. One by one she succeeded, just as, one by one, the decaying prefab houses on the estate where she lived were demolished—some were even set on fire by local kids. By 1963, Jane and her children were living in the last surviving house, now almost 20 years old. When it rained, the asbestos walls became porous and her children found a new game. 'Look Mum, we can push our fingers through!'

At least the walls of her French house were sound.

Jane's frugal approach was rewarded when a surprise cheque for £12,500 arrived, with a solicitor's letter explaining the money represented proceeds from the trust fund set up by her late grandfather. Her father had died and 'Pa' Ferdinando had been as good as his word. The solicitor went on to explain that Jane could also expect a small annual distribution from the Trust. She breathed a sigh of relief—there was no point grieving over the errant father she'd never really known—banked the money and got on with arranging essential repairs.

Lucien put pressure on the plumber who surprised them all by agreeing to foot the bill for any additional work, and Francoise found a workman who knew how to fix septic tanks. He came out, dug up the pipe work and discovered that road works had blocked the original drainage system. Solving the problem was simply a matter of laying a new pipe. The main roof was fixed, a prototype solar panel was fitted and workmen lined the ceiling of the grain loft. There wasn't enough money to decorate but at least the room was watertight and suitable for guests. Pam's early departure hadn't been forgotten.

The work was completed just in time for an onslaught of family and friends. Jane's eldest son, Clive—the bearded, astrology-loving engineer with a sense of humour to match his size—arrived with his wife Penny, and daughter Jenny turned up with granddaughters Gemma and Kate. Building work was set aside and there were day trips, outdoor BBQs and visits to and from the neighbours.

Any misgivings Jenny might have had about the wisdom of her mum moving to France seemed inconsequential as they basked in the back garden. enjoying a prolonged bout of sunshine. Jane said nothing about the times she felt lonely or depressed. She loved being mortgage-free and owning her own plot of land, she even loved the solitude, but there were times she craved the company of others and missed her family and friends more than she ever admitted. Jane set her concerns aside. There was no going back.

In mid August, when all the visitors had gone and life had quietened down, Jane took stock, trying to remember who it was who said nature abhors a vacuum. The grass had steadily advanced, suffocating all the tender young plants she'd put in. There was nothing for it but to fight back. She looped a belt around her waist, fixed it to the back of the chair and wheeled outside.

On the first day she snipped and clipped at swaying grass and weeds to uncover the lavender. On the second day she found the box and the astilbe and on the third day she got as far as the willow tree. Her back ached and her wrist throbbed as she sat in the garden nursing a nightcap, contemplating all that had been achieved in the past twelve months. A channel had been dug between the road and the back door—the start of a path that would one day circle the garden. Young plants had started to take root and the muddy field was gradually being colonised. The solar panel was fitted, the bathroom finally worked and the house was liveable at least.

It was time to celebrate. At the end of August, after a spate of hot, sunny days, Jane invited her neighbours for an aperitif. It was a double celebration to mark her first anniversary in Maca and her sixty-fifth birthday.

She put champagne, beer and white wine in the small bar fridge and set bottles of ginger beer and water on the table. She sliced bread, cut cheese, unwrapped pate and filled dishes with nuts, olives, crisps, biscuits and cherries. Time and again she wheeled outside, the tray on her lap piled with glasses, plates, napkins, knives, forks and spoons, each time unloading the contents of the tray onto the white plastic table that stood by the back door. As the afternoon wore on she swept out the veranda and dragged plastic chairs into place. When everything was ready Jane wheeled outside, closed her eyes and turned her face towards the sun.

'Bonjour Jeanne!'

Jane lifted her head with an effort, wiped the sleep from her eyes and squinted towards the smiling Lucien and his wife Therese.

'Bonjoor! Entrez! Now, what can I offer you to drink?'

Jeannine and Robert were on holiday but Francoise and Jean Yves joined the party with their children, Charlotte and Benjamin, along with Monsieur and Madame Lagueux and Alain Legros.

After a year of near-total immersion, Jane's French had improved to the point where she could understand most of what was said, and construct full sentences. She could finally chat to her neighbours, even if it did sound like she was speaking the Queen's English. The only one who defeated her was the smiling Alain, the dog-loving recluse who lived up the road, but neither he nor Jane were going to let something as inconsequential as language get in the way of enjoying an afternoon with friends and a glass or two of wine.

'I want to propose a toast to my new friends,' said Jane. 'Thank you for welcoming me to Maca and making me feel so at home.'

'Sante Jeanne!'

'Sante! Your health!'

It was late evening when Alain tottered up the road towards home and Francoise and Therese helped stack the empty glasses and dirty dishes in a laundry basket before carrying them away to wash. 'Don't worry Jeanne,' they shouted. 'We'll bring them back!'

Jane sat alone in the quiet garden after they'd gone. Twilight lingered, toying with the last few shades of indigo as the sky darkened and a swoop of bats appeared, flitting through the slender gap between night and day, dipping their wings in the inky sky.

11 SUMMER LOVING

Jane's appreciation of beauty wasn't confined to the natural world.

'A bronzed Adonis,' she whispered, staring at the suntanned profile of a young stonemason repairing a wall in the garden. She wheeled outside to offer the hapless object of her appreciation a glass of ginger beer and a garibaldi biscuit, admiring the muscles that rippled under his shirt and the way his hair curled at the back of his neck.

Jane had chosen to live in a tiny hamlet in a remote part of north-west France, but she had no intention of eking out her retirement in quiet obscurity. What would be the fun in that? She was full of life, she always had been. Anyone willing to look beyond the wheelchair could see that.

Her wish list in France included finding a French lover and when I first heard about Jane's plan I thought she was joking. 'Sounds wonderful,' I said. 'Can you find me one too? Make him tall dark and handsome. I'd like a rich aristocrat, preferably with his own chateau.' Jane went along with the joke but underneath the laugher she was deadly serious. There was fun to be had and life to be lived. At sixty-five, she hadn't given up the hope of meeting someone.

She had met plenty of married men, including Arnold, a stocky translator in his early 60s who spoke 26 languages, six officially as a freelance translator at the town hall. Arnold taught English at several local high schools and he translated Jane's birth, marriage, divorce and death certificates into French. With the demise of her second husband, Geoffrey, she had a full set. A generous man, Arnold often stepped in to help when she struggled with officialdom, and he always refused to take any further money. His serious demeanour masked a jollity that appealed to Jane but Arnold was in a serious relationship with Hannelore. Then there was the lovely Lucien, with his twinkling eyes and knowing smile, married to the equally lovely Therese. There was no shortage of married men but Jane had rules. Married men were off limits.

It wasn't that Jane lacked company. There were plenty of people who popped in. Her immediate next-door neighbours, Jeannine and Robert, were frequent visitors, Jeannine especially. There was the smiling Lucien and his elegant wife Therese, whose daughter in law Francoise and her husband Jean Yves were also regular visitors. Further afield in St Nazaire there was an American friend, Elise, and her husband, another Jean Yves, as well as children who came for English lessons.

In spite of all the visitors, there were times Jane felt lonely; she missed having a man around. She consoled herself, as she so often did, with gardening, drawing on the patience and determination that had seen her through challenging times before. Her approach to life in France was no different. When the time was right, she would set about finding a French lover, for now she carried on digging.

Most of Jane's neighbours were more used to growing food than flowers, especially those old enough to remember the restrictions of war and German occupation, but they recognised Jane's love of plants and happily donated cuttings for her to transplant. Monique brought a cutting of mimosa, which Lucien planted out. Someone else donated a tiny peach tree and Jane handed out tomato seedlings in return. The draughty plastic-covered veranda had found a use as a makeshift greenhouse, and earlier in the year she'd planted dozens of tomato seeds in old yoghurt pots, empty margarine tubs and cardboard tubes from old toilet rolls. They had all sprouted.

Jane planted anything that might help the 'soak-away' system, including a dwarf weeping willow, a cherry tree, silver birch, scented philadelphus and flame coloured broom. Each time she went shopping she kept her eyes open for plants that liked getting their feet wet. The trick was to buy them cheaply from the supermarket when they were about to be thrown out. Those that looked like they were dying could often be resurrected. Lavender, sage, mimosa and box went in, along with iris, begonia, hosta and astilbe.

The warmer weather encouraged a proliferation of grass and weeds and Jane was digging in the garden one afternoon when a chubby boy on a bicycle appeared at the side gate.

'Bonjour Madame. Je m'appelle Romain. Can I help?' he asked.

'With pleasure!' Jane called.

Romain's mum, Maryse, was consulted and she seemed perfectly content to let her eleven-year-old son spend his spare time at a stranger's house.

Romain's appearance prompted others to join in and soon a team of young helpers was recruited to try and bring order out of the chaos. They willingly earned extra pocket money in return for cutting grass, clearing weeds, moving rocks and cleaning windows. Romain's four-year-old sister, Marina, sometimes tagged along although she couldn't decide what she enjoyed most; helping the others or getting her big brother into trouble. Angelique Biore and her older brother Fredric were two more willing recruits to the gardening gang and Jane let her mind wander towards the day when curving paths might snake through the whole garden.

After months of digging, helped by neighbours, friends, visiting family and the indefatigable members of her gardening gang— including twelve-year-old Benjamin, who was mad on motorcars, and little eight-year-old Morgan—the first channel was at last complete. It ran from a small parking spot at the side of the house to the back door then along the back of the house. Another channel ran at right angles, starting at the parking spot, continuing along the side of the garden and heading all the way to the animal shed at the top.

The outline was soon blurred in places by fast growing weeds and grass, so Jane rang Benjamin to help her drop stone markers along the edge of the channel, indicating where the concrete would have to be poured. A concreting gang was already lined up. Sixteen-year-old Fredric Biore knew someone who could lend him a cement mixer and he and his school friend, Pascal, were eager to earn some extra cash. They were on standby to lay the path one weekend, as soon as the weather was fine enough.

It rained for the rest of September. The stone markers disappeared, swallowed up by swathes of grass that put on a vigorous spurt in the hot, wet weather. Jane knew it would have to be cut again before the concrete could be poured. Romain, the jolly boy on a bicycle who normally helped with mowing, was away, so Jane tied herself into her chair, picked up a pair of shears and wheeled across the uneven soil.

In places the grass was so high it reached the top of her wheels. She bent forward and began the attack. After an hour of cutting in the sweaty heat she looked up. She'd managed to clear about a metre. Undeterred she wheeled forwards, lurched into a shallow ditch and got her chair stuck on the uneven ground. It took a quarter of an hour of shifting, rocking, pulling and easing to drag herself free, and she paid for her efforts with a swollen hand that stopped any further cutting.

Two weeks later Romain returned and Jane rang him to ask if he could help cut the grass one more time.

'D'accord Jeanne.'

When Romain saw the sea of grass he dropped his bicycle and turned to Jane, eyes wide with disbelief. 'But Jeanne! Why haven't you been cutting the grass?'

Jane smiled. 'Because I've been waiting for you. Come on, let's get started.'

One misty Sunday morning in early October Fredric and Pascal arrived with their cement mixer. Jane parked Bijoux (as she affectionately dubbed the eight-year-old Metro she had driven over from England) across the road to leave room for them to work and she shut herself indoors. All day long the boys mixed and poured and shovelled and smoothed. A ribbon of concrete unfurled across the garden as they bent to their task. By midday the morning mist had burnt off and the sheen of wet concrete shimmered in the autumn sunlight. Pausing only for sandwiches and ginger beer they laboured on.

Eight hours later Jane had two new parking spots made from compacted sand, gravel and cement and a brand new concrete path leading to the back door. The path also ran around the side of the garden and all the way to the top. The boys were triumphant.

'Voila Madame Lambert!'

Jane was thrilled with the results. She paid the jubilant boys for their efforts and promised to cheer Fredric on in his cycle race the following weekend. Her neighbour Lucien thoughtfully tied a ribbon across the path to keep people from walking on it and Jane settled in for the evening.

Trapped indoors, she spent the time making bread pudding from a stale loaf of bread, squashing the soggy mix between her fingers. She scooped handfuls of the bread mix into a cake tin balanced on her lap then lowered the door of a mini oven—a recent purchase to supplement her basic kitchen—swung the cake tin up with both hands and hefted it into the oven. She had recently introduced her neighbours to the delights of English bread pudding and they all wanted more.

The following Sunday Jane got up early, drove out of Maca and parked the car where she knew she would get a good view of Frederic's cycle race. A blur of wheels zoomed past and she flapped a hanky out of the car window. She had no idea which bicycle Fredric was riding, or even if he'd seen her.

'Allez, Frederic!' she shouted.

Later that day she rang to find out how he'd done.

'I saw you Jeanne! You were waving a handkerchief.'

'Did you have a good race?'

'I came thirty-fourth.'

'Magnifique! Well done Fred.'

A flicker of movement caught Jane's attention at breakfast one morning and she stared hard at the floor. Moments later a ripple of fur scurried out from under the shelving unit and shot behind the fridge. Jane screamed, and the piercing noise alerted Jeannine. Moments later she was knocking on the back door, her worried face pressed against the glass.

'CA VA?' she called.

Jane wheeled across and pulled open the door.

'I found another mouse! Un souris!'

'Ah, oui.' Jeannine shrugged. Mice weren't that unusual in Maca, as Jane soon found out. In three days four more appeared. One shot out from under the sink, two ran out from behind the television and another disappeared under the washing machine. The sudden flutters of rapid movement terrified Jane. Each time it happened she let out a piercing scream and Jeannine would appear moments later at the back door.

'CA VA?'

Not surprisingly, Jane's next-door neighbour grew tired of the screaming and suggested poison. 'It is the only way,' she declared, 'if not, you will have an infestation. AN INFESTATION. Do you understand?' Jane understood only too well.

The poison did the trick and she disposed of several dead bodies but some of the village children who heard about the problem decided there was a better solution. The masterminds behind the conspiracy were ten-year-old Angelique Biore and her brother Frederic, both keen members of Jane's gardening gang.

'Madame Lambert, will you come and have tea with us tomorrow afternoon?' their mother Christine asked. 'The children have a surprise for you.'

Angelique, Frederic and his girlfriend Myriam were giggling with anticipation when Jane wheeled into their house. She spotted a cardboard box on the floor, partially hidden behind the laughing youngsters, and she guessed what was inside but played along anyway. 'Oh what have you got there?' she asked, wheeling forwards as the children nudged each other aside. Jane stretched a hand into the box and felt soft balls of fur tumble over her fingers. Angelique knelt down and picked up a mewling black kitten, its yellow eyes only just open. She placed it in Jane's lap. 'This one's perfect for you Madame Lambert,' she said, shyly.

'Look he loves you already,' said Myriam. 'He can catch all your mice!'

'And he'll be good company!' Frederic added.

It was true what the children said, a cat would be good company and it might even catch a few mice but Jane wasn't convinced. There was still a lot of work to do in the house and she'd been planning to get a dog one day, not a cat. 'I'll think about it,' she said, returning the kitten to its mother.

Any doubts Jane might have had were dispelled several days later, when she heard the black kitten with yellow eyes had broken its leg. Would anyone else in that part of rural France have bothered to pay a vet's bill for a six-week-old kitten? Kittens were easy to come by and marshes close at hand. As far as most residents of Maca were concerned it was easy come, easy go. But Jane could never turn her back on an animal in distress. She got rid of the poison and agreed to take the black kitten.

'What will you call him Madame Lambert?'

'I'm not sure. What about Michel? Or Robert?'

'You cannot Madame, he has to have a name beginning with L.'

'Why?'

'Because it is 1994!'

The children explained the French rules for naming pets. Each year a new letter was used, which meant dogs called Sam, Simone or Sarkozy were all the same age, older than Babette or Berenice. Jane decided to call the six-week-old kitten Leo. He'd proved his bravery and she was hoping for big things from her miniature mouser.

The vet in Savenay put a tiny splint and plaster on Leo's broken leg and the energetic kitten raced around the garden, his white splint flashing in the tall grass.

Jane kept digging and the tide of weeds kept advancing. If she looked at the overall picture any gains seemed insignificant. The answer was not to look. She concentrated on one small patch of soil at a time, and if she did raise her head it was to watch Leo, bouncing unsuccessfully after jays, house martins, gold finches, grey wagtails and wrens, all of them frequent visitors to the garden.

The children were right, Leo was good company, but he wasn't the sort of company Jane was hoping to find.

12 FRIENDS AND LOVERS

Market day in St Nazaire was always busy. Jane slowed down, searching for a spot to park. The roads were clogged with traffic and the pavements thronged with people. Stallholders lined the narrow cobbled streets, hidden behind stacks of plastic crates and wooden boxes. There was a pungent smell of cheese, an iron rich tang of blood and the scent of fresh garlic. Prices were scribbled in chalk on black slate markers and tucked into pyramids of tomatoes, onions, courgettes, potatoes, carrots and whatever else was in season. Freshly laid eggs, live chickens, rabbits, field mushrooms, bedding plants, shoes, hats, underwear, hardware…it could all be bought at St Nazaire market.

Jane normally went with her American friend, Elise, who lived locally and could help navigate the uneven streets. They would make a day of it and have lunch together afterwards, but Elise was heavily pregnant and not up to pushing a wheelchair. Jane decided to risk going alone. The French people she'd met so far had been overwhelmingly kind and if she got stuck she was sure a Good Samaritan would lend a hand.

The hardest part was finding somewhere to park—there were times she'd driven to St Nazaire and been forced to turn around and drive home again for lack of a suitable spot. Not today though. She eased the car into a disabled parking space with plenty of room at the side and winched down the wheelchair. Getting across the main road, with its steep pavements on either side, was more of a challenge. She positioned herself at a suitable crossing point and waited.

'May I help you Madame?'

Jane turned to look at the man standing behind her, who already had one hand on the arm of her wheelchair. He was in his mid 30's, with close-cropped hair, a stubble of dark beard and the warm brown eyes of an eager spaniel. Jane treated him to her most engaging smile. If all the Good Samaritans looked like him she was in for a good day. Maybe St Nazaire market would be a good hunting ground.

'Merci,' she beamed. The handsome stranger stepped off the pavement and Jane watched him cross the road without a backward glance, leaving her stranded and confused. Moments later another helper appeared. 'Madame, do you have need of assistance?'

'Merci!' She called over her shoulder, bracing herself as she waited for the stranger to grasp the handles of her wheelchair, tip it backwards and ease it off the pavement. Nothing happened. She looked back and saw him striding away in the opposite direction. When a third person appeared Jane took no chances.

'Madame, do you have need— '

'Oui! Oui! S'il vous plait!'

Firm hands tipped the wheelchair back and Jane was bumped down the pavement. She laughed and made a mental note. 'Merci' didn't mean thank you it meant no thank you.

Jane's dream of meeting a sexy French lover had so far yielded nothing more concrete than the odd flirtatious smile from a stranger at St Nazaire market. Her hope of meeting someone single and available in the depths of rural France might have seemed wildly optimistic to some people. Jane didn't think so.

She had embarked on the long and painstaking process of carving out a new life for herself, and she was determined to enjoy it. She was putting down roots, establishing friendships and getting to know the people, places and customs of her new country. That included learning a new language, renovating her house and planting a garden. Throughout it all, she relished the journey.

When she felt secure enough, she would look for a lover. She was in no hurry. She simply kept her eyes open, and she was ready to flirt at a moment's notice with anyone willing to look beyond the wheelchair. Even the experience of her good friend Barbara didn't put her off.

Jane met Barbara in the late 1970s, when they both belonged to a choir in South Ealing. Jane's second husband had just died and Barbara had recently gone through a messy divorce. She was a gregarious, statuesque woman a few years younger than Jane, with a thicket of dark hair piled on top of her head. As well as singing in the local choir together, they went to jumble sales and car boot sales, rummaging for bargains and gossiping over tea afterwards. Barbara had vowed to have nothing more to do with men. 'You and I both know men are overrated,' she declared, looking to Jane for confirmation. Based on her experience so far, Jane had to agree.

In late summer of Jane's second year in France, Barbara made a surprise announcement. She was planning to visit Jane and she wasn't alone, she had a new boyfriend in tow.

Jane made arrangements to pick them up from the train station in St Nazaire. She parked the car on the street outside and waited for the couple to emerge. When they did, Jane spotted immediately that something was wrong. Knowing Barbara as well as she did, Jane could see her friend looked drawn and uneasy. The man trudging beside her was staring at the ground, his fine blonde hair flopping over a high forehead. He looked up when Barbara pointed out the car and lifted his hand in greeting, smiling in a way that did nothing to shift the strain etched on his forehead.

The tension in the car was palpable on the drive back to Maca. The stifling midsummer heat didn't help and Barbara's new boyfriend, Peter, was unnaturally polite. They ate the simple salad lunch Jane had prepared in strained silence, broken occasionally by well-mannered conversation and desultory questions about France. As soon as lunch was over, Peter pushed his chair back. 'Come on Barbara, there's work to be done,' he said.

Jane knew Barbara was wilting and she wasn't surprised; there was no breeze to counteract the fearsome heat. All of them needed to rest. 'It's all right, leave the washing up,' she said 'We can do it later.'

Peter ignored Jane's advice. He made a show of doing the washing up, bustling around the small house, clattering the plates as he collected them and dropping them noisily onto the sink. 'Barbara, you're being lazy, Jane needs help,' he called across the room, his spare frame bent over the sink. Jane raised her eyebrows at her friend who silently shook her head.

Jane spent several days driving Barbara and her new boyfriend around, doing her best to keep them entertained. Peter was a fractious guest. *You're not paying attention Barbara. Why aren't you listening? How can you be tired? You stayed in bed half the morning, that's typical of you. Is that another cigarette? How many have you smoked now?* He seemed intent on putting Barbara down and Jane was surprised that her normally spirited friend didn't react. Why was she willing to put up with such behaviour? Jane wanted none of it. Whenever Peter made a disparaging remark she did her best to choke him off. In her opinion he was an obnoxious beast.

The trip culminated in an enormous row in the early hours of the morning as Barbara and Peter raged at each other in the grain loft above Jane's bedroom. She lay in bed, listening to their loud recriminations. As soon as it was light she heard Peter clump down the uncarpeted stairs.

'I'm not staying another second!' he shouted. 'I'll walk to the station if I have to!'

Jane heard the back door slam then the sound of footsteps crunching on the gravel outside. She got up and put the kettle on, waiting for Barbara to come downstairs. When her friend did emerge, her face was blotchy with tears.

'I'm sorry Jane I didn't mean to inflict this on you,' Barbara said.

'Don't be silly,' Jane said, hoisting a cup of tea onto the table. 'You're a good friend and it doesn't matter. I'm just worried for you, that's all.'

Barbara sat at the table, put her head in her hands and poured out her troubles. Jane did her best to be sympathetic but all she could think was, 'good riddance'. Barbara lit a cigarette and pulled a deep drag of smoke into her lungs. 'He's not always like that,' she said.

'What are you talking about? He was rude to you from the minute he arrived!'

'I know. Do you think I should go after him?'

'No. He said he wanted to hitch. Let him.'

Barbara stubbed out her cigarette and reached for another. 'We were meant to be catching the train to Paris this morning,' she said, checking her watch. 'It leaves in an hour from St Nazaire,' she added. Jane sighed. 'What do you want to do?' Barbara crushed out another cigarette, blew her nose and drained her cup of tea.

'Do you want to go?' Jane asked. Tears sprang to Barbara's eyes as she nodded glumly.

'Come on then,' said Jane. 'I'll drive you to the station.'

They spotted Peter en route to St Nazaire, trudging along the road and unsuccessfully trying to hitch a lift. He looked like an overgrown boy scout, a lonely figure stooping under the weight of a bulging rucksack. Jane pulled up beside him and the warring lovers made up, reconciling with tears and sobbing apologies.

She dropped them at the station in time to catch the next train to Paris and watched them walk across the forecourt. 'Have a great holiday!' she called, leaning out of the window as they turned to wave goodbye.

'Good luck, Barbara,' she added quietly. 'I have a feeling you're going to need it.'

In early December Jane used the last of Pa Ferdinando's legacy to fix up the annexe then she closed the interconnecting door to keep the cold from seeping through into the kitchen. The painting and decorating, flooring and installation of heating would have to wait a few months—or years—until she'd saved up enough money to pay for it.

Bundled into a thick woollen sweater to combat the chill that seeped in from the unused room, Jane began preparations for

Christmas. Over the course of several days she licked, looped and stuck hundreds of paper streamers together and late one afternoon Charlotte came over to help put them up. The agile young girl clambered onto a chair to reach the pendant chandelier in Jane's living room, clutching a long snake of paper streamers as a bundle of black fur leapt into the air. Charlotte snatched the streamers out of reach. 'Leo! Arrête!' She looped one end of the streamers around the light fitting and coiled the other end into Jane's lap.

'Jeanne, are you going to keep your hair that colour?' she asked, looking down at the top of Jane's head.

Jane laughed. 'Are my roots showing?'

Charlotte moved the chair to the other end of the room and fixed another line of streamers to the ceiling. 'I can do them for you if you like. I love hairdressing,' she said, diplomatically.

Jane's eyes sparkled. Having someone to help with the messy business of dying her hair would be a huge help. 'We could come to an arrangement,' she said. 'I could pay you to be my regular hairdresser. What do you think?'

'I'd like that,' said Charlotte.

'D'accord,' said Jane eagerly. 'We've got a deal!'

Charlotte stepped back to admire her handiwork. The room looked like a festive primary school, draped with multi coloured paper streamers and decked with dozens of Christmas cards. 'Parfait!' Jane declared.

There were no visitors from England that Christmas, but with so many friends in the village Jane wasn't alone. Over the next couple of days she made a huge Christmas cake, adding more and more ingredients to make it large enough to feed anyone who might pop in over the holiday period. By the time she'd finished it weighed several kilos and was far too heavy for her to lift. Jeannine came over to put it into the oven and Therese called in to take it out, several hours later.

On December 22nd Jane drove to the bustling market in Donges, pushing her way through the biting Atlantic wind to find small gifts of chocolates and sugared almonds for neighbours and friends. She called in at the library and unearthed copies of *Miss Marple* and *Papillon* on video and Tchaikovsky on CD then she drove home to make a final batch of ginger beer.

The next day, with the temperature dropping still further, Jane did the last of her supermarket shopping at Intermarché, buying enough to see her through the Christmas week. It was just as well. When she wheeled out to the car, bulging carrier bags balanced on the footrests of her wheelchair and on her lap, she discovered her wheelchair hoist had packed up. The troublesome Bijoux was playing up again.

Luckily for Jane, Christine and her daughter Angelique had spotted her in the supermarket car park. They waited while she shuffled across into the driver's seat then they folded her chair, loaded it into the boot of the car and followed her home to help unload at the other end.

There was no point trying to get the hoist fixed on Christmas Eve so Jane stayed at home—gas fire switched to maximum against the increasing cold—and spent the morning bottling ginger beer with Charlotte. Cries of 'Bonjour!' and 'Joyeux Noel!" rang out as first Elise and Jean Yves dropped in with Christmas crackers then Jeannine called with a gift of chocolates wrapped in a delicate lace net.

'Love your hair Jane,' said Elise.

'I've got a new hairdresser,' said Jane. She grinned at Charlotte, who blushed with pride.

That evening, with frost whitening the cars and stars visible above, Jane wheeled across to Therese and Lucien's for dinner, two bottles of champagne nestled in her lap. She was dressed in a shimmering top of blue, red and orange, with velvet trousers and green shoes, and for once, she arrived without mud caked on her wheels.

The six-course feast began with an aperitif of vintage port, roast almonds and flaked apple. Next was a seafood platter of oysters, prawns, winkles and smoked salmon, then came Coquilles St Jacques in a frothy cheese sauce, teamed with a delicate rose wine, followed by a filet of rare roast beef with fluffy potatoes and green beans, washed down with a glass of Bordeaux. Jane passed on the tempting cheese platter, resisting the ripe delights of Neufchatel, Pont L'Eveque, Roquefort, Camembert, Chèvre and Boursin, to save room for a slice of Buche de Noel, which was filled with chocolate whipped cream, rolled into a log and served, naturally enough, with champagne.

The traditional Christmas meal was consumed in high spirits, with plenty of laughter and several bottles of wine. Jane was persuaded to stay to watch ice-skating on television afterwards, and it was the early hours of Christmas morning before the party broke up.

'Joyeux Noel!'

'Dormez bien! Sleep well!'

'Merci mes amis!'

Frost crunched under Jane's wheels as she made her way home, her breath pooling ahead of her. She glided across the concrete, clutching a parcel of scraps for Leo who was sitting in the window, watching for her. She smiled at his worried face.

'Ca va!' She called. 'J'arrive!'

The moon shone brightly on the frozen grass and the new concrete path cut a ribbon of white through the frozen earth. She was tempted to take a turn around the garden but it was late and, in spite of the brandy running through her veins, it was also bitterly cold. There would be plenty of time in the coming weeks and months.

The next morning she woke to find the bathroom heater had packed up and there was frost on the inside of the windows.

Over the next few months I stayed in touch with Jane by letter, laughing at her dealings with a builder who mistakenly knocked down the crumbling pigsty in the back garden, commiserating with her about the car that kept breaking down and marvelling, as I always did, at her unending patience and her ability to see the funny side of every situation.

Summer lived up to its promise that year and the days were filled with endless sunshine. Atlantic sea breezes, so bitter and unwelcome in winter, brought relief from the stifling heat as the temperature approached 30 degrees and stayed there for two months. Jane spent most of her time outdoors.

Granddaughters, Kate, Vicky and Becky made a quick trip out for Easter and Jane whirled them around the sights, cramming in beach picnics, markets and supermarket shopping trips before driving them back to Nantes airport. Clive arrived with his wife Penny for a few days and Jenny called with husband Tim and family on their way to and from Provence. The sun shone and guests were willingly put to work. If rain stopped play it didn't last long—most of the time, the covers were off. Her little gardening gang worked hard all summer, nourished by copious amounts of lemonade and ginger biscuits, and by the end of the school holidays they had finished cutting another path through the garden.

Autumn approached and Jane kept digging and planting, planting and digging. She was adding to the garden, bit by bit. Each new patch of cleared ground was a victory against the tide of grass and weeds. Each new plant added a splash of colour or scent and often meant one less item she had to buy from the fruit and vegetable shop. Whether you can see beauty amongst the rubbish in life, or rubbish amongst the beauty, depends on your outlook. Jane noticed the fledgling plants flourishing amongst the weeds and she knew the scales would tip one day.

As winter fell she had fewer visitors. Cold winds and storms kept her out of the garden and she went back to the library for entertainment, doing her best to keep bleak thoughts at bay. She was fed up with being alone. In spite of the obvious difficulties of meeting someone she hadn't given up on the idea. She wanted company, male company, and it was time to do something about it.

13 WOMAN SEEKS MAN

Friends describe Jane as practical, optimistic, stubborn, cheerful and determined. She's all of that and more. There's a strong romantic streak in Jane's character. It's a romanticism that has more to do with nineteenth century ideals than fairy tales and storybook fantasies. Jane believed in the power of nature; she exalted music, art and beauty. She didn't just want to create a beautiful garden and a comfortable place to retire in, she wanted to experience all the joy, beauty and pleasure life had to offer, and that included finding a mate.

Who but a true romantic would embark on the adventure of a lifetime in their mid sixties? What sensible person would move to France, a country they'd never even visited, where they didn't speak the language, knew no-one and where they would have to eke out a small pension in a house best described by friends as near derelict? Who else would try to find love under such circumstances? Add disability into the mix and the challenge seemed insurmountable, the odds overwhelming.

Not for Jane. Never mind the wheelchair, never mind the age, the romantic side of Jane's nature drove her on, urging her to live life to the full. A lot of people in Jane's situation would have given up and quietly retired rather than face the potential ridicule and disappointment of trying to find love. Jane rose to the challenge. She refused to give up. She was prepared to climb her equivalent of the Eiffel Tower, spread her wings and launch herself from the top. If that's what it took, that's what she would do.

Jane's enthusiasm for life can make her feel like a character in an Enid Blyton novel. *Come on Timmy, let's dig for treasure over here!* Her optimism brooks no argument and her sunny disposition refuses to accept failure. Jane will commiserate with you when life deals you a bitter blow—as it does us all at times—but she sees no point in wallowing in self-pity. There's far too much fun to be had. She approached dating in the same way.

With Christmas looming, Jane rang her American friend, Elise. 'I'm looking for a man,' she said. 'What do you want him for?' Elise asked. Given that Jane was normally after a plumber, a builder, an electrician or a mechanic it was a fair question. 'I might leave that up to him,' she said. There was silence on the end of the phone until Elise caught up. 'Oh! You mean you want a *man*.' Jane couldn't help laughing. 'Yes. There are lots of nice men around here but they're all husbands of friends. They're off limits. I don't know how to go about looking for a man. I've never had to do it before.'

'I'll see what I can do,' said Elise.

Several days later a local paper turned up in the post. *Le Pelican* was a weekly newspaper produced in Nantes. Jane leafed through it and found it ran a letters page and a personal column. She read through the ads.

Mature businessman, financially successful, tall, dark hair, glasses, seeks younger female.

Married man searching for discreet companion. Must be willing to travel at short notice.

Passionate sportsman, looking for sincere, affectionate woman with a good sense of humour who likes sailing and travel.

There weren't any ads Jane wanted to reply to but it seemed like the perfect place for her own 'petite annonce'. Jane was thrilled to discover there was a relatively easy way of meeting a succession of prospective lovers and she couldn't wait to get started. She fully expected going on a blind date to be a lot of fun. She wheeled out to the garden, dropped her notepad onto the table and started writing.

English woman, retired and now living in France, interested in fine art, music and gardening, would like to meet someone, ideally bilingual, for social outings and help with reading a French newspaper.

It was carefully crafted and deliberately understated but the intention behind it was to find a French lover.

Christmas came and went and January brought its now familiar but no less depressing mix of frost, hail, sleet and rain. At one point it was even cold enough for snow. While Jane waited for a reply to her ad she decided to get a haircut. If she was going on a date she wanted to look good. Young Charlotte did a great job of dying Jane's hair but she couldn't be expected to cut it as well. Money was tight and hairdressers were expensive so Jane decided to do it herself. Anyway, she thought, how hard could it be?

Clutching a pair of scissors from the kitchen she wheeled into the bathroom, pulled her wheelchair as close to the sink as she could get it then leant forward and started cutting. She was aiming for a mid length bob. She snipped away, stopping occasionally to check her reflection. The fringe wasn't bad but the sides weren't level. She kept cutting, first one side then the other, and hair piled up in the sink as Jane kept cutting. When the shoulder length bob reached her ears Jane put the scissors down, sat back and looked in the mirror. The haircut was an unmitigated disaster.

Two days later a letter arrived, postmarked Nantes. She tucked her thumbnail under the flap and ripped it open.

Chere Madame,

We regret to inform you that we cannot accept the advertisement you wish to place in Le Pelican newspaper…

She puzzled over the letter, wondering what was wrong.

…not permissible to include your home telephone number. We suggest you establish a PO Box number at the newspaper.

So that was it. She would have to resubmit the ad and use a PO Box number instead. She rang the newspaper and learnt she'd just missed that week's deadline; the ad wouldn't appear for another two weeks. She consoled herself with the thought that at least it would give her hair time to grow out before she went on her first date.

The unremitting cold, damp, grey days threatened to plunge Jane into depression. Her spirits were at their lowest in the first week of February. It was freezing cold, far too cold to get out into the garden and she'd been sleeping badly. The solar hot water system didn't work on grey days and the wall mounted water heater, turned up to maximum to battle the freezing temperatures, rattled its way through the night, keeping her awake. The little cabine in the garden had flooded and the video recorder broke down.

On Sunday she felt so fed up she did nothing all day. 'It's too depressing,' she wrote on the calendar. The next day her spirits lifted. The *Le Pelican* newspaper arrived and her petite annonce was in. No matter that snow was falling from a grey sky, her campaign to find a French lover had begun! She marvelled at the sight of crocuses and camellias flourishing in the frost, smiled at a new bloom on the second stalk of her indoor orchid and tackled the housekeeping with renewed energy.

A week later Jane received two replies to her ad. The first was a letter listing the sender's virtues. It was a long list. He owned his own flat and he was neat and tidy, reliable, responsible, faithful, honest and true. Not quite the exciting lover Jane was after but never mind, he also liked DIY and there was plenty of that to be had at her house.

Undeterred by the self-righteous tone she rang 'Monsieur Too Good' and they arranged to meet for coffee the following afternoon at the local supermarket. She didn't say anything about being in a wheelchair. In spite of his admirable qualities, Jane had a feeling Monsieur Too Good might be put off and anyway, she reasoned, she wanted a lover, not a carer. The supermarket was a carefully chosen rendezvous, with plenty of disabled parking directly outside so Jane would have a sneak preview of anyone standing at the entrance while she parked the car. She was looking forward to the date with unbridled optimism.

On the morning of her first date Jane got up early and washed and dried her hair. It still looked ragged but it would do. She pulled on a midnight blue jumper, red trousers and draped a brightly coloured scarf around her shoulders to take the focus away from her hair. She applied eye shadow, mascara and threaded large hoop earrings through her pierced ears. Before she left she checked her reflection in the bathroom mirror and carefully applied a line of bright red lipstick. Not bad, she thought.

Things started to go wrong on the short drive there. She got stuck behind a 'convoi exceptionnelle'—an oversize, slow-moving truck. Overtaking was always tricky in a left hand drive car and Bijoux didn't have the best acceleration, so she was forced to stay behind the truck. When she pulled into the supermarket car park she was already ten minutes late.

She could see a man standing outside the entrance, checking his watch, but by the time she had lowered her chair from the roof, hauled herself into it, locked the car and wheeled across to the supermarket the man was nowhere to be seen. She hadn't seen him leave so she decided he had to be in the shopping centre somewhere. She set off to find him.

She had a quick look around some of the smaller outlets that ringed the supermarket and most were empty. None of the customers matched his description so she changed tack and positioned herself at the main entrance, hoping to spot him as he left. Five minutes later a short, slim, disgruntled-looking man—the one she'd spotted earlier checking his watch—approached the entrance. Head down, car keys in his hand, he clearly hadn't been shopping since he wasn't carrying any bags. Jane accosted him as he strode past.

'Bonjour Monsieur!'

He stopped, frowning, and she beamed at him.

'Je suis Jane!'

Jane watched the colour drain from his face and he stumbled over the introductions. Eventually she came to his rescue. 'Shall we go for a coffee?' she suggested.

They talked about family, home and holidays, but no amount of polite conversation could cover Monsieur Too Good's shocked reaction at seeing his blind date was in a wheelchair. 'I have to go away for a short while,' he said. 'I'll get in touch with you when I'm back.'

Jane rang Elise when she got home. 'He was a funny little man. He went white when he met me.'

'Had you told him about the chair?'

'No. I reckoned he wanted to meet me, not my wheelchair.'

'Will you see him again?'

'I don't know. He said he'd call.'

Jane turned her attention to the second reply, which sounded more promising.

Chere Madame

You are just the sort of woman I'm looking for…

She read further. The writer was clearly intelligent and articulate. He was a translator—that could be useful—and he worked at the local Palais de Justice. It all sounded very familiar and slow realisation began to dawn. Jane checked the signature at the bottom. The letter was from Arnold, the multi-lingual translator who had been so helpful when she had first arrived in France. Even now, Arnold often helped Jane when official documents and tricky situations defeated her. Arnold's wife had died several years ago and he now had a steady, live-in girlfriend. She checked his letter again.

I would be delighted to meet you. Perhaps I can help with your French.

She thought about ringing and decided against it. Instead she wrote back.

Dear Arnold

If it weren't for the fact that you already have a girlfriend, you might be just the person for me…

She signed her name at the bottom and smiled as she pictured his face when he opened the letter.

Monsieur Too Good didn't ring back so Jane rang him. 'Would you like to meet up again?'

'Ah…yes. Just for the moment, my children are visiting. Perhaps I can call you when I'm free?'

'D'accord,' said Jane, keeping her voice light.

In spite of the setbacks Jane didn't feel downhearted, quite the reverse. Where there had been two replies, there might be more. While she waited for those replies to materialise there was planting to be done. The shaky veranda looked like it was going to be with her for a while so she decided to put it to good use. It would serve as a warm spot for seedlings, if nothing else.

She potted sweet pea and cherry tomato seeds and started digging a new vegetable patch outside. Even when the car broke down—again—it didn't dispel her good humour. Bijoux had recently been consigned to the garage with an oil leak, and it was the latest in a long line of repairs. The silencer had gone, all four tyres had been replaced and the car had taken several knocks. Driving an English car on the wrong side of the road hadn't improved Jane's skill behind the wheel.

The mechanic, Jean Claude, rang to pass on the latest news. 'Bonjour Madame Lambert, we have discovered the problem with the car.'

'That's good, what's wrong with it?'

'Unfortunately you have need of a new gear box, Madame.'

'That sounds expensive.'

'Normally, yes. I can try and find a second hand—

'Yes please!'

—but you know Madame, we don't have so many Rover cars here in France.'

Jane rang her son Clive in London. 'Bijoux needs a new gearbox. Any bright ideas?'

'I'll try and find a reconditioned one.'

It turned out to be easier than expected and it only cost £150. Only. That was more than Jane had in the bank so she rang her son Roger and he offered to lend his mum the money. The problem of getting the gearbox to France was solved when friends Sally and Jim announced they were making another trip over a few weeks later. They were coming by car, so they could bring it with them.

Word soon got around that Jane was without a car and a fleet of helpers sorted out shopping, banking, post and trips to the library.

One Sunday afternoon while she was stuck at home, young gardening enthusiast Romain called in with his girlfriend, Doris, and they brought a French board game, 'La Bonne Paye', to help while away the time. A mix of snakes and ladders and Monopoly, the goal was to avoid huge bills and be the player who accumulated the most money at the end of the game. The trio spent a couple of hours playing and, needless to say, Jane didn't win.

With Bijoux in the garage, Jane relied on visiting shopkeepers for provisions. The fishmonger was typical of the fastidious French approach to food. He pulled up one morning in a van as surgically white as his coat then he clambered out of the driver's seat and walked through to the back. The side of the van was lowered to reveal a gleaming display of herring, skate, mussels, cockles, bream, cod and octopus, nestled on a pristine bed of parsley and ice. The fishmonger tended the display as he waited for customers to appear, heaping ice onto the mussels, turning a swordfish steak so it showed to better advantage. Jane sat in her open front doorway, trapped by the raised sill, and waved at him. He waved back and proudly spread his hands above the display of seafood.

'Alors Madame. Qu'est-ce-que vous voulez?' he called.

'Do you have six Coquilles St Jacques?'

'Coming right up Madame!'

The fishmonger wrapped the scallops in white paper, climbed out of the back of the van and walked across to deliver them to Jane, the smell of the Atlantic Ocean seeping through his fingers.

A few days later Jane received a phone call. 'Bonjour Jeanne! Ca va?' She recognised the voice immediately. 'Hello Arnold, how are you?' she replied. 'C'etait une blague!' he said. 'A joke! We both knew it was your ad. Both of us! Ha ha!' Jane detected a nervous edge to his laugh. 'Is that right?' she said. 'But of course!' She went along with the joke, although she suspected it was Arnold's way of getting out of trouble.

She couldn't resist sharing the story with Jeannine when she popped in later that day, and they swapped stories of misdemeanours over a pot of tea. When Christine called in, carrying armfuls of pinks she'd dug up from her garden, she found them helpless with laughter.

Without a car Jane couldn't arrange any more dates, although as it turned out she needn't have worried. After the first two letters there were no more replies. Monsieur Too Good didn't call again and it looked like putting an ad in the personal column had been a costly failure. Jane consoled herself, as she so often did, by gardening.

By mid April Jane was mobile again. Ever optimistic, she decided to give Monsieur Too Good one last chance. Maybe she'd been too hasty in writing him off, it was always possible he'd mislaid her number. The Easter Fair at Nantes was coming up and Monsieur Too Good lived in Nantes. What better opportunity to meet? She rang his home number and the answering machine clicked on.

'Bonjour! It's Jane. I'm going to the Fair at Nantes this weekend. I was just wondering if you were going. If you are, perhaps we could meet up?'

Monsieur Too Good rang the next day and made it clear he didn't want Jane to contact him again. She ripped up his letter and threw it away.

Allez, en route! Behind the wheel in France.

Listening to Handel's Messiah, rugged up against the cold.

Early days at the front (new window on the right).

Early days at the back (solar panel installed on the roof).

Gardening gang distracted by kittens.

Laying the new concrete path.

The author with Jane at her dining room table, 1996.

With René at the same table, 1998.

René gets his just desserts in the kitchen.

Fauvette was one stray Jane couldn't turn her back on.

The beautiful Benji, adopted after Fauvette died.

Pierrette, the third cat Jane adopted.

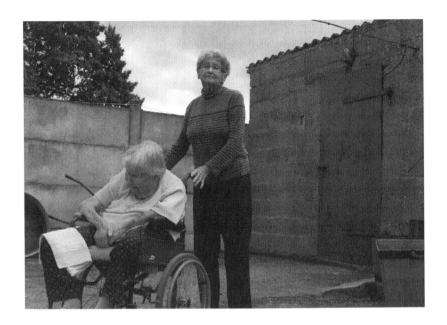

Jane and her next-door neighbour, Jeannine.

Francoise and Jean Yves.

Centre of attention at her 80th birthday celebrations.

Members of Jane's extended family made the trip over to France.

There's always something to be done in the garden.

And Jane is always eager to do it.

The flourishing back garden today.

The front of the house today.

14 MAN SEEKS WOMAN

With the help of her loyal team, Jane attacked the field at the back of the house. Angelique and Morgan worked on the site for the new pond and Jane planted sweet pea and tomato seedlings. Romain helped transplant evening primrose and Charlotte swapped her hairdressing scissors for the lawnmower to help Lucien cut the grass. Together they moved rocks, shifted barrows full of mud, dug up weeds and scrubbed garden ornaments clean.

They planted lily of the valley from Monique's garden and tiny peach trees donated by the builder. They sank lily rushes into the borders of the new pond, potted carnations, added peppermint to the herb garden and pulled up weeds as fast as they appeared.

There was no suggestion of using weed killer to stem the tide. In Jane's view enough wild flowers had been eradicated through the overuse of chemicals already; she wasn't about to add to the destruction. She paid for her principles with painful hands that throbbed with arthritis.

May was wet, cold and miserable but June made up for it with a breezy heat wave that exhausted Jane's scant reserves of water. Her team of gardeners turned into a Fantasia-like relay of helpers, carting buckets left under the shower and watering cans filled from the dwindling water butt. Jane didn't use a hosepipe. The most she would do was supplement natural rainfall with hand watering; if a plant couldn't survive the summer largely unaided, it wasn't meant to grow in her garden.

As summer approached, last year's dahlias showed their heads. The clematis bloomed and so did the roses. Jane spotted kestrels, magpies and turtledoves flying through the garden. A pair of swallows took up residence in the petite cabine and late one night there was the unmistakable sound of a frog croaking. At last, she had a weapon against slugs. Butterflies, moths, crickets, lizards and bees thrived, and an eggshell dropped to the floor of the old pigsty as the swallows busied themselves feeding their growing family. The heat increased and rain seemed a distant memory.

Jane harvested a bumper crop of fat tomatoes and distributed them to neighbours. Children came for English classes and friends called in for lunch. Lucien, the man who seemed as strong as an ox, was taken into hospital and Jane called in to see Therese, bearing tomatoes and ginger beer as a gift. Everyone in the village worried about him and there was relief all round when he was discharged ten days later, seemingly none the worse.

When it was too wet to garden Jane went to art exhibitions, lectures, flea markets and concerts in the church at St Nazaire. Wherever she went she kept her eyes open. She was determined to meet someone and this was the year to do it.

At St Nazaire market one Sunday she spotted a man standing on his own, handing out leaflets. She'd seen him a couple of times before, normally on his own and always handing out the same leaflets. She took one and stopped. 'Bonjour Monsieur.' He looked surprised that anyone should want to stop and talk. 'What are you campaigning for?' Jane asked.

'Refugees,' he said, with a quick sideways glance to see how Jane might react. 'People in France who have no papers,' he added.

'Is that a big problem in France?' Jane asked.

'Yes.'

The man seemed reluctant to talk and he kept his eyes lowered, refusing to look directly at Jane. He gave the impression of a man defeated by life. His loneliness was tangible and Jane felt sorry for him, as she did for any lost soul, but such a man wasn't for her. She bought a bag of peaches and a clump of white petunias and went home to plant them.

Fauvette was one lost soul in the village Jane couldn't turn her back on. A woolly mongrel with round hazelnut eyes, light brown ears and a matching backside, Fauvette was a stray. She looked more like a grubby white lamb than a dog. Her owner, an elderly man who lived alone on the outskirts of the village, had died and Fauvette had been left to run wild. No one wanted her. She roamed the village, begging for scraps and barking at anyone who approached. Jane couldn't help noticing that she also wagged her tail at the same time.

When Christine turned up at Jane's house to peg out washing one day, Fauvette followed. Jane stayed indoors and watched the stray dog snuffle through the compost heap, searching for food. The dog looked skinny and half starved, prompting Jane to put a bowl of cat food outside the back door.

Fauvette approached warily, waiting until Jane was back inside before she swallowed the food in a single, choking gulp. Jane watched quietly from the kitchen as Fauvette sniffed the open back door. The wary dog barked, wagged her tail and wiggled her brown bottom. 'Come on then,' said Jane.

Fauvette hesitated. She paused on the threshold, sniffed the air then walked through the open door and approached the wheelchair. Jane reached down and placed a hand on Fauvette's hot woolly head.

'Hello little one. Are you looking for a new home?'

Leo wasn't impressed. He gave Fauvette a tooth and claw reception, trying everything to repel the intruder until Jane let the cat assert his superiority and sleep on her bed. A truce was called when Leo found he liked dog food and Fauvette accepted she would be eating cat food from now on.

It took Fauvette a while to work out she had a permanent home. Each time she escaped, young Angelique brought her back. She and the other members of the gardening gang adored Fauvette, and dog washing the woolly bundle became their favourite new chore. After yet another chase through Maca, Angelique and her mum, Christine, helped tie Fauvette up more securely in the garden.

Jane assumed it was safe to leave her and she drove to the local town hall to watch a dance show in which one of her English students was performing. When she got home, at nine o'clock that night, Fauvette was nowhere to be seen. Jane set off in search, whistling and calling the dog's name.

'Fauvette! Viens! Viens ici!'

Her calls were ignored. She was still searching at one o'clock in the morning and knew she couldn't continue the search much longer. A local couple, Crystelle and Fabrice, was getting married in the morning and she'd been invited to attend. As it was she'd have to get up at the crack of dawn to have any hope of finishing the card she'd been painting to go with their present.

She spent another fruitless half hour, calling and whistling, until she was forced to give up and go to bed. Wherever she was, Fauvette would have to fend for herself. Jane set the alarm and fell into a deep sleep.

She was finishing breakfast the next morning when there was a familiar bark at the back door. Christine stood outside holding a lead. 'Get down Fauvette!' said Christine, as a woolly head and a pair of muddy paws appeared at the glass. Christine sounded irritated and she looked tired. Jane opened the door and Fauvette bounded in.

'Merci Christine. Where did you find her?'

'She was outside on the street and she's been crying all night. She is a very bad dog. You are a very bad dog!' said Christine sternly. Fauvette wagged her tail, gulped down a bowl of cat food then slumped onto a cushion in the corner of the kitchen and fell asleep.

When Jane arrived at the church later that day she was met by a succession of bleary-eyed people, all with the same complaint.

'Madame Lambert, is your dog asleep yet?

'What was your dog barking at? She kept it up for hours!'

'We didn't get a wink of sleep last night thanks to that mongrel.'

Jane had slept through it all. She apologised to each disgruntled guest and promised not to let it happen again. Less than a week ago Fauvette had been a stray; now she was quite firmly Jane's problem.

Buoyed by the sunshine and long hot days of early summer Jane planted potatoes, cucumber and peppers. She also decided to make a renewed attempt to find a lover.

'I'm doing it the wrong way around,' she said to Jeannine.

'Doing what?'

'The ads. Looking for a man. I'm going to start answering them instead.'

So one breezy Saturday in early July Jane drove to Donges and she bought a copy of the local paper. She went home, made a cup of tea and sat in the garden reading the personal column. There were four possibles, all living in and around Nantes. It was a forty kilometre trip from Maca to Nantes but that wouldn't matter, since the reconditioned gearbox had been fitted Bijoux had been running well. She circled the ads she was interested in.

Educated mature man, interested in fine arts and music, seeks like-minded partner.

Financially solvent businessman, late 60s, looking for attractive companion.

Retired academic, lonely, wants to meet someone for friendship and possible long term relationship.

Older gentleman with youthful spirit searching for lively woman to share fun times together.

She drafted a standard reply that she hoped would suit all four.

Cher Monsieur

I read your advertisement with interest. I'm a mature woman with red hair and blue eyes. I enjoy fine arts, gardening and history. I moved to France when I retired two years ago and I now live in a cottage near Donges. My French is improving all the time! If you are interested in meeting up please call me on ...

The next day she hand wrote individual copies of the letter to all four men. On a whim she wrote out a fifth, for a man in St Nazaire, which was only twenty kilometres away. He was searching for *la perle rare*. I'm certainly a 'rare pearl' thought Jane, and she couldn't help laughing. Nothing ventured, nothing gained. She drove to the post office with Fauvette on Monday morning and sent all five letters.

Driving back from Donges she approached a junction and pressed the hand lever that operated the brake but instead of the usual bite of resistance she felt her hand sink into a soft pillow. She pulled in to the local garage.

'Bonjour Madame. How can we help you?'

'The brakes on my car seem—

Jane searched for the word.

—like cake.'

'Spongy?'

'Exactly!'

The mechanic crawled under the car while Jane waited in the driver's seat. She heard tapping under the floor and moments later he reappeared, wiping his hands on a rag, which he tucked into his overalls.

'Madame. The problem is serious. I am sorry but I will need to keep your car.' Jane sighed and pressed the button to release her chair from the roof. 'May I use your phone please?' she said.

Christine came to her rescue, pulling onto the forecourt in a car big enough to take a wheelchair. Jane spotted Angelique and Morgan waving enthusiastically from the back seat, their faces pressed against the window.

'We've come along in case you need any extra help,' said Angelique, climbing out of the car and setting off a barrage of barking from Fauvette.

'Good idea,' said Jane. Fauvette was encouraged to jump into the car and Jane positioned her wheelchair next to the open passenger door. 'Christine you stay in the car and Angelique and Morgan, if you both stand behind my chair I'll tell you what to do.' Jane reached across to grab the passenger seat with one hand and the handle of the door with the other. 'Now, Angelique and Morgan, when I count to three, I want you to push hard on my bottom, and Christine, you pull me towards you at the same time.'

'D'accord Jeanne!'

'Right. Here we go. One, two, THREE!'

Jane hauled, the children pushed, Christine pulled and Fauvette barked furiously as Jane was dragged into the car. Christine packed the wheelchair into the boot and the children squashed into the back, giggling and screaming as Fauvette licked their faces and leapt from one lap to the other.

On Thursday the garage rang to say the car was ready and Robert drove Jane to the garage to pick it up. The bill for repairs came to far more than it had cost to have the gearbox replaced and Jane wrote out a cheque with a shaky hand, hoping her overdraft would cover it. She drove home and poured herself a stiff drink, followed by another.

However low she felt that Thursday it was forgotten on Friday when a cheque arrived from the solicitor charged with looking after her grandfather's estate. The distribution of funds from the trust was just enough to cover the cost of repairs to the car. It was uncanny how just enough would turn up whenever she needed it most. According to her daughter Annabel, it was something to do with Jane having Pluto and Venus in her second house. Whatever the reason, the funds were a welcome relief. The phone rang later that afternoon.

'Madame Lambert?'

'Oui'

'Bonjour. My name is Jean Francois. You sent me a letter.' The chocolate-rich voice was soft, low and seductive. Jean Francois oozed charm. It was obvious he knew how sexy he sounded and Jane happily played along. 'Meet me tonight,' he whispered. 'Seven o'clock. Le Temple. I know an excellent restaurant. Very private. Very intimate.'

Jane hesitated. Le Temple was over thirty kilometres away, past Savenay, on the route nationale heading towards Nantes. It was a long drive, and she had no idea what the disabled access would be like when she got there, probably not good. Somehow she didn't think Jean Francois was the type of man who would want to meet in a supermarket car park.

'D'accord!' she said, smiling with anticipation. She hung up, wheeled into the bedroom and began rummaging through her clothes. Jean Francois sounded like one sexy Frenchman and she was going to go all out to impress.

While she was deciding what to wear, the phone rang again. The caller introduced himself as Edmond, another of the prospective lovers Jane had written to. He had an educated voice and a far more subtle approach.

'I'm keen to improve my English,' he said. 'Would you care to have lunch?'

They arranged to meet at the local Castorama supermarket the following Wednesday, where there was plenty of parking and a disabled loo.

It had been a hot day and the evening promised to be fine. Jane took her time getting ready. She chose a silky blouse, patterned in red and gold, and soft trousers in palest green. She added earrings and bright red lipstick then smiled at her reflection in the mirror. Her hair had grown and it framed her face well. Her blue eyes sparkled.

'Be good,' she sang out to Leo and Fauvette, as she wheeled out to the car. It was a lovely sunny evening and her spirits were high.

There was hardly any traffic on the main road and it was an easy drive. She arrived early, found a parking spot, unloaded her chair then pulled herself into it and wheeled over to sit on the sunny side of the car while she waited for Jean Francois to arrive.

Ten minutes passed and Jane checked her watch. Fifteen, then twenty minutes trickled past. Had she made a mistake with the time? No, he'd definitely said seven o'clock, she'd written it down. By half past seven she knew she might as well go home. Jean Francois wasn't coming. Had he driven past, seen the wheelchair and kept going? Probably.

Jane shifted back into the car, loaded her wheelchair into the top box and drove home. Perhaps there would be a message on the answering machine. She checked the phone when she got back, looking for the tell-tale flashing light but there was nothing. Jean Francois didn't bother to call to explain and she never heard from him again.

Edmond rang the next day. 'Let's not wait until next week,' he said. 'What are you doing today? Could we meet?' Jane put her disappointment over Jean Francois to one side and agreed to meet Edmond for coffee in the local McDonald's.

She arrived early, which meant she was sitting at one of the tables when Edmond walked in. He looked much older than he sounded. He admitted to being seventy-eight but Jane suspected he was probably a lot older. She couldn't help thinking he seemed a bit dull but there were two things in his favour. If he was surprised at seeing the wheelchair he hid it well, and he liked DIY. 'I can keep you busy,' Jane said with a laugh.

It turned out Edmond was an old hand at answering ads in personal columns. He regaled Jane with tales of other women he'd met and Jane revised her opinion. Maybe he wasn't so dull after all. 'Shall we meet again?' she asked.

'Ah, my family is staying with me at the moment. Let's meet after they have gone. I'll call you.' Jane wondered if she was being given another brush off. 'Yes, my family is coming to visit too,' she said. 'Why don't you give me your number, that way we can stay in touch?' She took Edmond's number and they promised to speak again in September.

The five letters Jane had written generated one more response, from Joel, the man looking for his 'rare pearl'. They arranged to meet at the Hotel Korali, near the train station in St Nazaire.

She left with plenty of time for the short drive to St Nazaire and was relieved to find the disabled parking spot directly in front of Hotel Korali was free. She unloaded her chair, retracted the hoist, shifted across from the car then fitted the hand and foot rests and wheeled towards the hotel.

The lobby was snug, just big enough for a reception desk in one corner and a couple of armchairs positioned under the window. The man sitting in one of the chairs matched Joel's description so Jane wheeled towards him, confident that her newly washed hair and carefully applied make up did her justice. The man looked up and Jane smiled. She saw his eyes register the red hair and he frowned. He looked beyond her then looked back.

Jane grinned. 'Yes, it's me. Jane! Bonjour Joel.'

Joel stood up and took a step back, as if Jane were carrying a disease he might catch. 'You didn't tell me you were disabled,' he said, shuddering as he looked at the wheelchair.

'You didn't ask,' Jane snapped back.

'It's impossible,' he said. 'Impossible.' And he walked away.

Jane wheeled out to the car, shifted across into the driver's seat, lowered the hoist, packed the chair away and drove home.

15 CONSEQUENCES

'Pity the rare pearl who ends up with him,' Jane muttered, dismissing the ill-mannered Joel. She wasn't going to waste time lamenting the loss—his, not hers.

Jane could easily have fallen into a depressive slump but she chose not to. In her opinion, if a date didn't work out there was no point clinging to disappointment. Much like a reliable London bus, she was convinced there would be another man along soon enough.

She replied to two more ads, and while she waited for a response, she made arrangements to visit the annual Fête de la Mer in St Nazaire. The two-day extravaganza was being held to celebrate the centenary of the launch of Le Belem, a famous sailing ship. With shipbuilding St Nazaire's main industry, it promised to be a spectacular show.

The sparkling harbour was crammed with two, three and four-masted sailing ships, and a flotilla of small boats including dozens of 'pointus'—tiny fishing boats pointed fore and aft.

Orange flags on a circus tent fluttered in the wind like goldfish gasping for breath. Passers-by were beckoned with the promise of jugglers, tightrope walkers and spectacular gymnasts. There were food stalls, sideshows, unicyclists, live music and fire-eaters. Much of it was inaccessible to someone in a wheelchair so Jane parked the car close by, wound down the window and enjoyed the spectacle.

A few days later the flotilla of tall ships was due to sail up the Loire to Nantes. Jane told her neighbours she was planning to drive out to a viewing point near the refinery, in case anyone wanted to join her, and Christine, Angelique and Romain accepted the invitation. On the day in question, Jane got up before dawn, packed a surprise picnic breakfast for everyone and drove them out to the headland, where she parked the car and they watched the graceful display float past as the sun rose over the horizon.

The following week she received two calls. The first was from a gentleman called Auguste and they had a very proper, rather stilted conversation. He promised to call again and Jane wasn't surprised when he didn't.

The second call was from Guy, a local businessman. Guy was a widow in his early seventies, still working, and keen to find a partner. There was a definite spark as they flirted on the phone and plenty of laughter during their long conversation. Jane knew she'd caught his interest. They arranged to meet in a park next to the Town Hall.

Guy was attractive, lively and a great talker, and Jane was more than a match for him. The spark had been ignited and she suggested they meet again. 'I'll call you,' he said as they parted.

When he did call it was to let Jane know he thought she was too old for him, he wanted someone younger. She put the phone down, disappointed. 'Stupid old fool,' she muttered. 'If you were willing to settle for less it could have worked.'

Fauvette was having more luck. One afternoon in late summer Jane took her on a walk through the village, her lead tied firmly to the arm of the wheelchair, and as they passed the last house Fauvette struggled free. Jane tugged her back but she was no match for the woolly dog. Fauvette arched her back, wriggled free and ran off into the bushes.

'Fauvette! Viens! Viens ici!' There was the sound of a brief scuffle and Fauvette reappeared several minutes later, wagging her tail.

By mid September the consequences were clear. Fauvette was pregnant and due to give birth any day. Jane put a cardboard box on the bedroom floor and she turfed a disgruntled Leo off her bed. Leo sulked in the kitchen, where his misfortune was added to when a stray cat barged through the cat flap and scoffed his dinner.

Between four-thirty and six-thirty the next morning Fauvette gave birth to a litter of six puppies. Jane recognised at least two local fathers in them. A muddy coloured mongrel that skulked the fringes of the village—the 'Beast from the Bog'—was responsible for at least two of the darker pups and the local chasseur's dog probably fathered the white ones. The others could have been anyone's.

English lessons were interrupted as most of the children from Maca called in to see the new arrivals. Angelique, Morgan, Romain, Maryse, Maryvonne, Paulette, Therese, Benoit and Francoise were among the stream of visitors.

'Regarde les petits!'

'Ils sont si mignon!'

What the children said was true, the puppies were cute, but the ever-practical Francoise wasn't swayed by such considerations.

'Jeanne, what will you do with them?' she asked.

It was a good question. In six weeks Jane would have to find homes for them. The visitors were all asked to spread the word and Jane gave the puppies English nicknames—Big Boy, Patch, Brownie—until they were old enough to open their eyes and have their sex confirmed.

Members of the gardening gang called nearly every day, offering plenty of advice on feeding and toilet training. Not much gardening was done. They were more interested in cuddling the puppies.

'Madame Lambert, this one looks like a pirate!'

'Madame Lambert, can I keep this white one?'

'Look Madame Lambert, that tiny one is getting squashed!'

The puppies nuzzled happily into the cups of the children's warm hands and the weeds in Jane's garden steadily increased their hold.

The last of the house martins flew the nest in late autumn and the weather turned chilly. Angelique helped pack away the garden furniture and Jane switched on the gas heater in the living room.

One by one, the puppies all learnt how to get out of the box they'd been born in and the days blurred into an endless round of cleaning and mopping. Romain helped fashion a makeshift cage from an old fireguard, which worked until they learnt how to wriggle underneath. In the middle of the night Jane would be woken by the plaintive cries of a puppy that had wormed its way out of the box, under the cage and was now shivering on the cold stone floor. She had no option but to grab the edge of the mattress, pull herself upright, shuffle into her chair and wheel over to rescue the distressed puppy.

Night after night she was woken at three o'clock in the morning as the puppies took it in turn to crawl out of the box, plop onto the floor and cry for help. Fauvette slept soundly in a corner, unmoved by their cries.

Noisette, Nelly, Nestor, Nicolas, Napoleon and Nazaire turned into wriggling bundles of trouble. The cleaning routine intensified and Jane's attempts to turn the veranda into a playroom met with limited success. Not a night went by without at least one of them waking up and demanding attention. Weaning couldn't come soon enough for Jane. At four weeks they could lap milk, at five weeks they were on milk, porridge and baby food, and by week six they managed mincemeat, Weetabix, pasta, beef and veal. Adorable though they were, it was time for them to go.

Jane heard of a woman in the market who wanted a puppy so she drove out to see her, clutching an envelope of pictures, but no, the woman had changed her mind. She drove home and spent another two hours sweeping and mopping.

Ads in local shops and in the local paper yielded better results. Three young people came to look at Nestor and agreed to take her. A nurse who looked after an elderly woman in the next village chose Nicolas and Madame Tartare took Nellie. Eventually there was just Napoleon left and a family who had lost their dog agreed to take him. Jane, Fauvette and Leo dropped back into their old routine. The temperature dropped, the wind sprang up and suddenly it was time to buy the ingredients for Christmas cake again.

Jane woke one morning having dreamt about Edmond, the elderly DIY enthusiast she'd met earlier in the year. He had promised to call in September after his visitors left and it was now late November and

Jane still hadn't heard from him. She took the vivid dream as a sign that she should call. What did she have to lose? He could only say no.

'Bonjour Edmond, it's Jane here, we met—

'Ah oui! Bonjour Jeanne! Ca va?' He seemed genuinely pleased to hear from her. They chatted easily and Edmond suggested lunch. 'Come to my place on Sunday. I'll cook for you,' he said.

Edmond turned out to be an excellent cook. Lunch was washed down with plenty of wine and 'dessert' was an unexpected treat. Jane left in high spirits, having invited Edmond to her place for a return match the following Sunday.

During the week she drove into Nantes in search of a new seat for her wheelchair. The problem with seats was always finding one sturdy enough for her to spend all day sitting on it yet flexible enough to fold when she stored the chair on top of the car. She loaded her second chair as back up, in case it was needed for spare parts.

There were plenty of good seats in the shop. Like Goldilocks, she tried them all. One was too soft, another too narrow; a third didn't have enough padding. When she did find one that was right the screw holes were in the wrong place to fit the frame of her existing chair. In the end, she got the technician to swap the wheels from her second chair with the wheels on her original chair. The second chair had a more comfortable seat and it would have to do.

While she'd been in the shop the weather had deteriorated. It was raining hard when she left and she struggled against the rising wind on her way back to the car. By the time she had shifted from her wheelchair to the car she was soaking wet. Visibility dropped on the drive back and the windscreen was pelted with needles of rain and hail. She got lost trying to find her way out of Nantes, a city she'd visited many times before, and by the time she got home it was blowing hard. Gale Force nine again.

Jane sat in the car, hoping the storm would die down. The plastic roof on the veranda creaked and groaned as it clung resolutely to its frame. Inside the house she could hear Fauvette barking furiously. There was no let up in the barrage of hail being driven against the car and the barking intensified. Fauvette knew she was out there.

Jane had no choice but to get soaked again. She went through the slow process of shifting from the car into her wheelchair as rain and hail drenched her clothes. By the time she reached it, the back door was jumping in its frame and her hands were so cold she dropped the key twice before she could get it in the lock. Once inside she barricaded the doors, fed the animals and went to bed to warm up.

On Wednesday Jane substituted Eric's English class with an hour-long cookery lesson, following an English recipe for Christmas cake so Eric could practice his English at the same time. The class produced delicious results. On Thursday the family who had lost their dog arrived to claim Napoleon and on Friday Jane went shopping for Sunday's meal. She decided to splash out. She bought oysters, scallops, cheese and champagne and came home to give the house a thorough clean.

On Saturday Cedric tacked more plastic over the chilly bathroom window to try and cut out the cold and Charlotte came over to do Jane's roots in the afternoon.

'What's he like Jeanne, the man you're having lunch with?'

'He's funny and very, very sexy.' Jane winked in the mirror and Charlotte dissolved in a fit of giggles.

Midway through Sunday morning the phone rang.

'Jeanne! Bonjour.'

'Bonjour Edmond. Ca va? What time do you think you will arrive?'

'Jane I am so sorry, there is a problem. I forgot to fill up with petrol last night.'

'Oh dear, will you be late?'

'The garage is shut. I will have to cancel our lunch.'

'Cancel? But surely we can -.'

'What can I do? I am stranded.'

'I can come and pick you up.'

'Ah non, non, non! I don't want to put you to any trouble. I'm sorry Jeanne. I will call you, another time.'

Jane recognised a brush off when she heard one, especially one so thinly disguised. She hung up, knowing she wouldn't hear from Edmond again.

On Monday morning, refusing to be downcast, Jane bought the local paper and scanned the personal column. There were two more possibilities. One was a retired foreman, seventy-two years old, who said he was looking for 'les relations amicales' and the other was an older man, looking for a lively companion. She wrote to both of them.

The temperature dropped and Lucien called around to stick tape around the doors to help cut down the draughts in the living room. 'Alors, Jeanne, any luck with the personal ads?' he asked. Jane shook her head. 'Not yet, but I haven't given up hope!'

Three days later the phone rang.

'Madame Lambert?'

'Oui.'

'Je m'appelle Michel. You wrote to me.'

'Ah oui.'

'Do you have large breasts?'

She put the phone down and crossed Michel off the list.

16 MISSED OPPORTUNITIES

By half past four in the afternoon the sun had long since disappeared. Darkness pressed against the un-curtained windows of the veranda as Jane sat at the kitchen table, rugged up against the cold, preparing for another English lesson. Michael had just left and she had a break of ten or fifteen minutes before Eric arrived.

The lessons didn't bring in much. Most were given in exchange for something else, like gardening, dog washing, window cleaning or help around the house, all things Jane would struggle to achieve on her own. The company counted for a lot though. In the depths of winter when the ground was frozen and birds had flown south she didn't go out much.

Plant catalogues kept her sane. The kitchen table was littered with them, pages open at glossy images of marigolds in bloom, carnations, dahlia, honeysuckle and sweet peas. Catalogues devoted to old-fashioned scented roses and flowering fruit trees had been pored over time and again, the pages dog-eared from use. The catalogues were a symbol of hope, a touchstone that stopped her giving up on the dream of building a new life in France. They took her attention away from the dwindling finances and cold weather that slowed her down and kept her shut indoors, her sluggish muscles struggling to cope.

Clive had rung earlier to say he'd bought three young apple trees, promising to bring them out the following March. They would give the garden more shade, more structure and, one day, abundant crops of autumn fruit. One day. Jane held to her future plans with grim determination.

The phone rang again and she wheeled across to answer it, glancing at the clock. Maybe Eric was calling to cancel his lesson. She wouldn't be surprised. A nasty dose of flu was doing the rounds and most people in Maca had suffered a bout of it.

'Allo?'

'C'est René. Tu rappelles? You wrote to me.'

'Ah oui! Bonjour René.'

She'd almost forgotten the last ad she'd replied to. She thought back to what René had said. It was fairly innocuous, something about being retired and looking for 'les relations amicales'—a friendly relationship. 'I'm glad you called,' Jane said.

'I'm glad you wrote.'

René's voice was deep and confident, with a strong accent Jane couldn't place. She thought back to what he'd said about where he lived. Nantes? St Nazaire?

'I'm trying to remember where you live,' she said.

'St Nazaire.'

'Your accent doesn't sound local.'

'Ah non. I am Parisian,' he said proudly. 'You are not local either.'

'You can tell?'

His laugh was loud and easy. 'You did not say in your letter how old you are,' he said.

'I'm sixty-eight.'

'That is good. And you are healthy?'

Now it was Jane's turn to laugh. 'Yes, I'm very healthy,' she said. It was true. In spite of the polio that confined her to a wheelchair her general health was good. René's direct approach was refreshing. He wasn't wasting any time so neither did Jane.

'What do you look like?' she asked.

'I am tall, dark and handsome. Seriously, I do not joke. Why be modest if you have nothing to be modest about?' he added. Rene went on to explain that he was one metre eighty-six centimetres tall, that he had dark hair and he wore glasses.

There was a knock at the back door and Jane looked up to see

Eric waiting outside. Fifteen minutes on the phone had passed quickly. 'I'm sorry one of my pupils has arrived. I teach English lessons.'

'Maybe there's something you can teach me? I'll call you later.'

True to his word René rang again that same evening.

'What do you like to be called? English Jane? Or French Jeanne?'

'I'm used to people calling me Jane.'

'Ha. Then I shall call you Jeanne. Ma Jeanne.'

His cheeky flirtation was audacious and challenging. He spoke quickly and decisively, often lapsing into argot, a Parisian slang that baffled Jane. René was just as mystified by Jane's attempts at pronunciation and there were times they barely understood what the other was saying but there was no mistaking the flirtatious laughter that lay just below the surface. René had none of the usual formal French 'politesse'. He was the kind of man Jane liked, the kind of man she'd like to meet.

'Do you drive?' René asked.

'Yes, I do.'

'Good. Because there is no point going any further if you do not drive. I can but I choose not to. And have you got a car?'

'Yes, René I do have a car.'

'Excellent.'

René was arrogant, opinionated and autocratic. He was also sexy, spirited and great fun. He liked sparring on the phone and Jane was more than a match for him. They hadn't made arrangements to meet but Jane was sure it was only a matter of time.

She got on with preparations for Christmas, sketching a pencil drawing of Fauvette and Leo curled up in the garden, adding bunches of holly and mistletoe to the scene. Francoise photocopied the sketches at work and Jane hand wrote Christmas messages on the back of each copy, carefully folding each one into four and slotting it into an envelope, turning the sketches into makeshift Christmas cards. Another expense spared.

René called again on Friday and his flirtatious comments grew bolder.

'A woman of eighty-two replied to my ad,' he said.

'Oh yes?'

'I thought, what's the point? What can you do with an 82-year-old?'

'That depends on the 82-year-old.'

René loved Jane's spirited responses to his outrageous comments and he was eager to meet. 'What about Sunday?' he said. 'The market will be on in St Nazaire.' It was an obvious choice of meeting place for René, who had no transport—the market was within walking distance. Jane hesitated. The market was outdoors. It had been raining on an off all day and it didn't look like clearing any time soon. She hadn't heard the forecast for Sunday, but if the weather in two days time turned out to be anything like today she'd get soaked just getting in and out of the car.

'Well?'

She'd have to take a chance. The market wasn't ideal but she was eager to meet. 'I can be there at eleven o'clock.'

'Do you know Laiterie de Menhir?'

'The cheese stall?'

'That's the one. I'll meet you there. How will I recognise you?'

If Jane was going to tell René about the wheelchair, now was her chance. She hadn't told any of her previous dates and most had reacted badly. She fought against having to mention it. The wheelchair was an irrelevance to her, why should it matter to anyone else? She was perfectly capable of living independently and if René was as keen as he claimed to be then the fact that she was in a wheelchair shouldn't matter a jot. She decided to say nothing and let them meet first. She wanted him to see that being in a wheelchair made no difference to her ability to enjoy life.

'I've got red hair,' she said.

'Ah fantastique, my little red head!'

'And I'll wear a blue coat.'

'Eh bien. See you Sunday, Jeanne.'

'A bientot.'

Jane put the phone down and made a quick calculation. This close to Christmas the market would be busy, especially on a Sunday. She'd have to get there early to be sure of finding somewhere suitable to park. They were meeting at eleven o'clock. It would take at least an hour to wash and dress, fifteen minutes to get into the car, half an hour to drive to St Nazaire then she'd have to find a parking space, fifteen minutes to get out of the car, five minutes to get to the stall. She totted it up. That was at least two hours. She'd have to be up well before nine o'clock.

She turned her attention to the bedroom. With the prospect of a hot date in a couple of days now was a good time for a clear out. Napoleon had been picked up a few days ago—the last puppy to go—and she was relieved to have found homes for them all. Adorable though they were, she wouldn't miss the constant mess and lack of sleep. She bent forward picked up the cardboard box the puppies had been raised in and carried it through to the veranda. It would be recycled later.

Fauvette whined and Jane wondered if she was still upset by the disappearance of her litter. The restless dog was lying on a cushion in the kitchen, watching Jane sweep out the bedroom. Fauvette got up, prowled around the kitchen then flopped back down as if she couldn't get comfortable.

Jane finished cleaning and began searching through clothes on her rack, wondering what to wear for the rendezvous on Sunday. She had a good feeling about René, although given the previous disasters she didn't want to get her hopes too high.

'What do you think Fauvette, hm?'

Fauvette got up and stretched her bum in the air. An ominous noise, like water swirling in a tank, gurgled from the dog's stomach. A moment later she jerked her head forward and vomited a stream of yellow liquid. Jane sighed and wheeled out to the veranda to fetch a mop and bucket. So much for the end of the puppy cleaning routine.

At two o'clock the next morning Jane woke to the sound of

Fauvette whining and scratching at the back door. She hurriedly dragged herself out of bed and into her chair but by the time she reached the sorry looking dog, there was another pool of curry coloured liquid spreading across the floor. The stench was overpowering. Jane did what she could to clear it up and went back to bed.

The next day, Saturday, Fauvette flopped around the house with a hot nose and sorrowful eyes. The only student was Angelique, who arrived at the back door looking as glum as Fauvette, with a streaming cold Jane didn't want to catch. She cancelled the lesson and packed Angelique off with a bottle of Vick's Vaporub.

Hoping to save time the next morning Jane showered and washed her hair and went to bed early, exhausted by lack of sleep. Fauvette prowled the kitchen, whimpering as she tried to settle, and her plaintive cries kept Jane awake until the early hours of the morning.

It was already light when Jane woke up and she hurriedly looked at the clock. Almost nine. Time to get moving. She pulled herself towards the edge of the bed and shuffled across into her chair, listening for Fauvette who would normally be outside the bedroom door by now, tail wagging, waiting to be fed.

She found the feverish dog lying on a cushion in a corner of the living room. Fauvette barely lifted her head when Jane went across to check on her. There was no need to check the veranda though, she knew what to expect from the smell.

'Don't worry Fauvette, it's not your fault,' she said, reaching for a mop and bucket and a bottle of disinfectant. Sloshing water over the floor she tried to mop up the mess, there was no way she could leave without clearing it, and precious time passed as she dragged the bucket into the bathroom, refilled it and mopped some more. The twin smells of dog shit and disinfectant clung to her and she knew she'd have to shower again before she left.

It was half nine before the floor looked vaguely clean, ten fifteen before she was out of the shower and dressed. Dry biscuits and fresh water were all she dared risk giving Fauvette and Leo. The disconsolate dog watched as Jane added a dash of red lipstick, grabbed her bag and pushed her wheelchair through persistent drizzle out to the car.

The chair hoist seemed agonisingly slow and by the time she was reversing out of the drive it was already a quarter to eleven. Sunday morning drivers and Christmas shoppers were everywhere. 'For heaven's sake get a move on!' she muttered to an elderly couple dawdling ahead. She gripped the steering wheel, swerved past a slow lorry, joined the short stretch of motorway and drove towards St Nazaire at the car's maximum speed.

The market was already busy with shoppers. At just after eleven o'clock she joined a line of traffic prowling the car park, willing the disabled spot to be free. Luck was on her side. She parked, opened the car door and pressed the lever to release her chair from the box, watching it creep down with infuriating slowness. She checked her watch. Ten past.

The wheels appeared above the door and she reached out to steady them as the chair swung sideways, hitting the car door on its gradual descent. The moment the wheels touched down she unhitched the lever, pressed the switch to retract the hoist and shook the chair open.

The hoist inched its way up into the top box and the box tipped sideways with yoga like serenity. It crawled back into place, and only then could Jane switch off the engine and shuffle across into her chair. She reached behind the front seat for the arm rests and foot plates, secured them into place and locked the car door.

Twenty past eleven.

The cheese stall was mobbed with customers and the canopy over the stall dripped drizzle as Jane confronted a wall of wet trousers. She lifted her head and accosted likely looking tall strangers.

'Excusez-moi Monsieur. Vous êtes René?'

'Ah non Madame.'

'Pardon Monseiur. Vous vous appellez René?'

'Non. Désole Madame.'

Jane pushed her way through the crowd until she was close enough to attract the attention of the stallholder. 'Excuse me Madame, do you know a Monsieur called René?'

'Tall man, with glasses?'

'Yes! That's him.'

The stallholder handed a parcel of cheese to a waiting customer. 'Trente cinq francs, merci Madame.' She turned her attention back to Jane. 'Yes, I know Monsieur René.'

'Have you seen him today? We were supposed to meet here.'

'I saw le monsieur just a moment ago.' The stallholder looked around and shrugged her shoulders. 'I am sorry Madame, I do not see him now.' Jane nodded, trying to suppress her rising disappointment. 'Merci Madame,' she said, turning away.

Had René seen her approach and quietly slipped away? Had the wheelchair put him off? He'd sounded so keen and confident when they spoke on the phone, would he really have been put off so easily? Jane wondered if she should have told him. If she had, he might have hesitated and made some excuse not to meet. Then what? No, whatever the outcome, she'd done the right thing by not telling him. But what was she going to do now? She didn't have a mobile phone and neither did René so there was no way of contacting him.

She set off on a tour of the market, searching the faces of other shoppers, hoping for a spark of recognition in someone's eyes. After almost an hour of looking she gave up. It was obvious she wasn't going to find him there.

She made her way back to the car and followed a line of traffic crawling out of St Nazaire. Rain spat against the windscreen and she turned the car heater up as far as it would go. The journey to the market had been fuelled by optimism and an excitable sense of urgency, the drive home was miserable. What was the point of all those hours they'd spent talking and flirting on the phone if the mere sight of a wheelchair was enough to put him off?

She swallowed the lump in her throat, parked the car at the back of the house and made her way through dull drizzle to the back door.

Fauvette greeted her with a healthy wag and Jane reached down to stroke her head. 'You feel better then. I'm glad someone does.' She checked the answering machine, just in case, but there were no messages and no missed calls. There was nothing to do but change out of her wet clothes and pour herself a consolation whisky.

The phone rang later that afternoon and a familiar voice boomed out of the receiver. 'Madame. This is René.' There was none of the playful flirting they'd enjoyed earlier in the week. Instead his voice pulsated with barely contained fury. 'We had a rendezvous!' he declared. His attitude could only mean one thing—he thought he'd been stood up. Jane felt a surge of relief that it had been nothing to do with the wheelchair.

'I'm so sorry. Fauvette, my dog, was ill. I was up half the night and I had to see to her in the morning so I was late leaving. I looked everywhere but I couldn't find you.'

René wasn't to be mollified so easily.

'I waited 20 minutes,' he growled. Patience clearly wasn't one of his many attributes. 'What a shame you couldn't have waited a little longer,' she snapped back, not bothering to hide her irritation. 'I looked for you for an *hour.'* René backtracked and they both calmed down. At the end of the conversation René suggested they make another arrangement to meet.

'I'll have to see how Fauvette is,' said Jane.

'What about Thursday?'

'That would be good, if Fauvette's better. If she's not I might need to take her to the vet. Can we talk later in the week?'

'D'accord. I'll call you.'

By Thursday Fauvette was well and René had rung several times. Each time their conversation became more intimate and more personal. By now Jane knew René's wife had died several years before of a brain tumour. He had three grown up children and was estranged from two of them. Jane still hadn't said anything about the wheelchair and she was feeling increasingly uneasy about it. René had shared many personal things about his life and she was keeping hidden something that impacted on everything she did. René was pushing for an answer. When were they going to meet?

'I want to meet my little redhead,' he said. 'Tell me where and when. I'll be there.' Jane couldn't bear to go through the disappointment of watching him react badly if the wheelchair took him by surprise.

She took a deep breath. 'René, there's something you should know.'

'What's that my little red head?'

'Many years ago I had polio. I use a wheelchair. If that's a problem for you, you'd better tell me now.'

She shifted in her chair. If the tone of his voice changed, if he made excuses or tried to suggest they meet another time, she'd know. Still, better to know now than find out when they met. It would be deeply disappointing, but she'd been through worse. The pause stretched into silence and Jane wondered if she had misjudged the strength of the connection between them.

'Do you still enjoy sex?'

The question was so unexpected she burst out laughing. 'Yes!' she said. 'I'm very partial to oats.'

'Oats?'

'Don't worry, I'll explain when we meet.'

'Good. It is not important, this wheelchair. My mother was a nurse. My father had curvature of the spine. Disability is nothing new for me. So, when are we going to meet?'

'Come for the weekend.'

René hesitated. He wasn't sure if he'd understood. 'Did you say let's meet at the weekend?'

'No, I said let's meet this afternoon and you can stay for the weekend.'

'Bravo Jeanne!'

17 OATS

When she stopped to reflect on the wisdom of inviting a complete stranger to stay for the weekend Jane phoned her next-door neighbour and told her she had met someone.

'He's coming to stay for a few days, you might want to pop in and meet him,' she said, knowing Jeannine would be powerless to resist. Jeannine would spread the word and a host of curious visitors would descend, but better that than be left alone with a complete stranger in a potentially tricky situation. What if he turned out to be an oddball? What if she wanted to get rid of him and couldn't?

Jane cleaned the house, tidied her bedroom, fed the animals and set off for St Nazaire at half past eleven, half an hour before she was due to meet René. Traffic was light and it was an easy journey. It was impossible to suppress a growing bubble of excitement. She'd slipped a bottle of champagne into the fridge before she left and it felt like she'd already downed a glass or two. Approaching the station she passed Hotel Korali, scene of the disastrous encounter with the obnoxious Joel. Whatever happened with René it surely couldn't be as bad as the date with Joel.

Ten minutes ahead of time Jane turned off the main road and pulled into the pickup spot outside the station. A tall man with broad shoulders, his dark hair peppered with grey and wearing gold-rimmed glasses was standing at the entrance. He wore a dark suit, highly polished black shoes and a woollen scarf tied firmly around his neck. A leather weekend bag was planted squarely at his feet. The stranger carried an air of authority, the authority of someone used to attracting attention. It had to be René. Even from a distance he looked confident.

He spotted Jane, picked up his bag and walked towards the car. Before she could wind down the window René had opened the driver's door.

'Jeanne!' he declared, thrusting his jaw into the car. Dark green eyes and full lips loomed towards her and she moved to kiss him on both cheeks in the formal French 'bise' of greeting. René had other ideas. He kissed her on the lips, with passionate intensity.

Jane felt like she'd been thrown into a swimming pool on a blisteringly hot day, an instant shock followed by a flood of sensation. If anyone else had done that she would have been furious, but she came up for air and grinned. René calmly walked to the other side of the car, opened the door, put his bag on the back seat and climbed into the passenger seat.

'Shall we go?' he said.

Jane reversed out of the station car park. 'What do you eat for breakfast?' she asked, regaining her composure. 'Whatever you eat,' said René, now grinning as well. They stopped at a supermarket and Jane stocked up on yoghourts, fruit, milk and bread before driving back to the house in Maca she had poured so much time and energy into.

The house had undergone dramatic changes since Jane had moved in. Walls had been knocked down and rebuilt, a basic bathroom and kitchen had been installed and patches of the garden had been colonised with plants. Someone who'd seen the house when Jane first bought it would have noticed those improvements. To an outsider, seeing it for the first time, it looked like a work in progress, with few obvious signs of much progress.

In early December the garden Jane was working so hard to create resembled little more than a muddy field. There was plastic tacked over the bathroom window to keep out the cold, masking tape to stop draughts in the living room, the rickety veranda with its plastic roof still clung resolutely to the side of the house and the only form of heating was still the portable gas stove.

Jane could see the potential in the house and she knew it would all happen one day. Whatever condition it was in now, it was the place she called home, and besides, the way it was developing suited her creative, colourful, optimistic approach. Jane had accumulated things too, like bags of zips, worn cushions, old trousers, empty yoghourt pots, broken pottery and the insides of toilet rolls, all of which could one day be used or recycled. What's more, most 'things' were out on display, within easy reach.

Jane knew a lot about René from their phone calls. She knew he'd been born and raised in Paris during the war. He'd worked as an engineer all his life, first in France and later in North Africa when there was no work to be had in France. He lived in a small terraced house in the centre of St Nazaire, a bustling town of over 70,000 people, and he liked living there. What Jane didn't know was that discipline and order governed René's life. He needed them, as surely as a plant needs sunlight and water, in order to feel secure and comfortable. He was orderly, sentimental and regimental, a traditional man who believed a woman's place was at her husband's side, raising children, preparing meals and looking after the home. It was her job to keep the home spotlessly clean, neat and tidy.

They unloaded the car and sat at the dining room table, momentarily losing the easy flirtation they had enjoyed on the drive over. Jane hadn't missed the signs of René's unspoken disapproval as she showed him over the house—not that he had tried too hard to disguise it.

'Would you like a cup of tea?' she asked.

René shrugged. He had never drunk tea before in his life. He normally drank coffee.

'If you like,' he said.

'Milk?'

Another shrug. René had no idea if you were meant to take milk in tea.

'OK,' he said, wary now.

'Sugar?' Jane asked.

René nodded vigorously.

'Two,' he said, no doubt working on the theory that if it tasted horrible he would at least sweeten it.

The tea went down surprisingly well and they moved on to wine, which went down even better and helped reignite the spark between them. Neither was interested in eating a meal so they had a light supper and went to bed.

Polio can weaken muscles to the point where they no longer function but it doesn't affect the sense of touch. Jane wrote a satisfied note on her calendar the next day. 'Both very tired'. She didn't worry that René might see it, he only knew two sentences in English. 'Zere is a book on zee tabul,' and 'My taylorr is reeche.' His bizarre English accent rivalled Jane's French for its sheer incomprehensibility.

The gas bottle ran out while they were having breakfast and Jane explained she would normally ring Lucien to ask him to pop over and change it. The alpha male in René rose to the occasion. He placed both hands flat on the table, raised himself to his full height and lifted his head.

'I shall do it,' he declared. 'Show me where it is.'

For all his height and bulk René wasn't as strong as he looked. He dragged the spare bottle from the veranda and heaved it into the living room. The colour rose in his face as he struggled with the heavy weight. He grunted, blew out his cheeks and swore under his breath. The operation took some time to complete. Later that day they drove to the local Castorama and Jane bought a wrench and trolley for carrying gas bottles.

Jeannine had a proprietorial interest in Jane's wellbeing, coupled with a burning curiosity to see who the stranger was and she waited until Saturday afternoon then could wait no longer. As soon as Jane answered her knock at the back door Jeannine stepped inside, head swivelling like an anxious mother hen.

'Bonjour Jeanne! I wonder if—oh, I'm sorry, I didn't realise you had company.' Mother Hen twitched her head in a show of feigned surprise and Jane tried not to laugh. René looked up from where he was sitting at the dining table.

'Bonjour Madame.'

'Bonjour Monsieur.'

'René, I'd like you to meet Jeannine, my next-door neighbour. Jeannine, this is René.' After the requisite amount of polite conversation Jane despatched Jeannine with a reassuring nod and Jeannine turned at the back door to give a discreet thumbs-up. Francoise went through the same routine two hours later.

Several weeks before René's unexpected stay, Jane had made plans to attend a dance performance at the local school. She knew some of the young performers and was keen not to miss it. 'You don't have to come if you don't want to,' she said to René. His chin rose. 'I will accompany you,' he declared.

Curious eyes followed their progress when Jane entered the town hall with a tall stranger in tow. She was well known by most people in the audience and René found himself shaking several hands. Jane busied herself greeting friends and the next time she looked up René had found a seat amongst the crowd. He had a small child perched on his knee. 'J'adore les enfants,' he said, beaming at Jane.

Sunday was a lazy day of sleeping late followed by brunch and a couple of glasses of wine, before Jane drove René home at five in the afternoon, just after it got dark. She pulled up outside his house—approached by a set of steps that made it impossible for her to go in—and they kissed goodbye in the car; a passionate repeat of their first greeting.

Jane drove home in high spirits, smiling all the way. What a weekend. It had been a risk, inviting him to stay the first time they met, but it was a risk that seemed to have paid off. René was a good-looking, sexy, challenging lover. He was great company, he wasn't afraid of the wheelchair and he made no concession for her disability. What's more, because he didn't drive Jane wasn't dependant on him; it was the other way around. They made each other laugh, they'd had a good time together and there was no doubt in Jane's mind that she wanted to see René again. Just the thought of it made her smile with anticipation. She hoped René felt the same way.

They spoke every couple of days, flirtatious and engaging conversations that reinforced the spark between them but they made no further plans to meet. With Christmas less than two weeks away Jane took the initiative.

'What are you doing over Christmas?' she asked.

'Pas grand chose,' said René. 'I will be at home, as usual.'

René was estranged from two of his children and the third lived too far away for him to visit. Jane knew he wasn't looking forward to spending Christmas alone any more than she was.

'Why don't you come here?' she said. 'Come and spend a few days here with me.' It was a typically generous offer and René was quick to accept.

Jane arranged to pick René up on Christmas Eve, a bitterly cold day marked by spitting needles of sleet. Cards and decorations added a festive touch to her house but, with no carpets on the floors and doors that rattled in the wind, it was far from cosy. Even at its maximum setting, the small gas fire in the living room struggled to create a pool of warmth that extended beyond a metre or so. René's carpeted townhouse in St Nazaire would have been snug and warm by comparison.

Is that when it started to go wrong? Did René realise, the moment he arrived, that he had made a mistake in accepting Jane's invitation? Did he suddenly wish he'd stayed at home? In retrospect perhaps they should have known better. They were relative strangers who'd met on a blind date three weeks earlier and they were attempting to spend Christmas together, a season loaded with meaning, emotion and expectation.

Unlike most Frenchmen of his age, René didn't believe in the authority of the Catholic Church—he thought Catholicism was a waste of time. Christmas wasn't a religious time for him, it was a time when families were meant to come together. This was family time, and René was estranged from his. There's no doubt he would have been comparing the experience at Jane's house with times past, when his wife had been alive and they would have spent Christmas with their children in familiar, comfortable surroundings.

Jane would happily have struck Christmas off the calendar; the pressure to have a good time, and the focus on elaborate meals, were all too much for her. She would far rather nibble on a piece of cheese and sip a glass of whisky than endure hours spent preparing turkey and all the trimmings.

The rituals of French family life, which so often revolve around food, were important to René and never more so than at Christmas. And as an old fashioned conservative, René wasn't about to lend a hand in the kitchen. He was steeped in Parisian male pride and he didn't see the need to help with the cooking or do the washing up. He did what he'd done all his life. He sat down at the table and waited for Jane to serve him a meal. His only contribution was to open, and sample, the wine.

With limited mobility in her arms and hands, cooking wasn't easy for Jane. Hours spent reducing a red wine sauce, making fresh hollandaise or simmering a bouillabaisse were out of the question, and peeling and chopping fresh vegetables was hazardous and time-consuming. Frozen vegetables were easier, and more practical.

René made absolutely no concession for Jane's disability. Was that because he saw Jane as a woman, and not a disabled woman? Or was it because of his innate sense of superiority? Whatever the reason, Jane wasn't worried about his lack of sympathy, quite the reverse. She found it attractive.

After years in hospital and rehabilitation, when others had taken control of her life, and later, when her husband had refused to allow her to drive, she'd craved independence and the chance to make her own decisions and control her own life. However well intentioned most people were, from medics to family and friends, Jane had always been on the receiving end of care. Decisions were made for her. Now here was someone who simply let her get on with it, and criticised her when her efforts didn't live up to his exacting standards.

'It's artificial rubbish. Jesus wasn't born in the winter solstice, that was just church politics,' Jane said, clattering pans in the kitchen while René sat at the dining room table, draining a glass of red wine and pushing the remains of a beef stew around his plate. 'He would have been born between the first and the twenty-second of August when the occlusion between Venus and Jupiter would have created a very bright star. That's what the wise men followed. There's always politics behind religion. Look at the old popes, decrying Luther, dying of syphilis.' René poured another glass of wine.

Their spirited conversations grew heated—put a liberal-thinking artist with a traditional Parisian and there are bound to be disagreements. As the days passed René grew increasingly fractious and he wasn't the kind of man to keep his feelings to himself. He was bad tempered and it showed. A couple of days after Christmas René suddenly declared that he didn't want to make love any more. Jane was devastated.

'Why? What's wrong?'

'I don't want to talk about it.'

'Is it something I've done?'

'No.'

'René, is it something I *haven't* done?'

'I told you, I don't want to discuss it!'

René retreated behind a curtain of bad tempered grumbling and Jane struggled to cope with the dramatic change. The next day he was openly offensive, insulting both Jane and her nationality. 'The English know nothing about food. You know nothing about culture. Look at this place, it's—'

'That's it! Stop right there! You can forget New Year. Get your things!'

No matter how attracted Jane might have been to René she wasn't prepared to put up with such obnoxious conduct. She drove him back to St Nazaire in mute fury, so angry at his behaviour she couldn't bring herself to speak to him. She had invited him to stay for

Christmas, welcomed him into her home and he'd done nothing but criticise, throwing all her efforts back in her face. If that was his attitude he could go back to his pristine, neat little house and turn into a bitter twisted lonely old man for all she cared. She never wanted to see him again.

René spent the journey slumped in the front seat like a petulant child. They completed the drive in silence, neither one willing to speak, and when she pulled up outside his house Jane turned to face him.

'It's over,' she declared. 'Termine! Do you understand? We don't have any sort of relationship, certainly not one that's amicale!' She took the words he'd used in his ad and threw them back at him. 'Adieu!' she said with finality. René picked up his bag and shuffled away from the car.

Jane had endured years of bullying, selfish behaviour and she wasn't going to put up with it ever again. If that's what René was like, he could forget it. She wasn't about to let herself be dominated or dictated to by anyone.

She blinked away tears of frustration as she drove home, her heart pounding. Their first weekend had gone so well, she couldn't understand what had changed. Why was René so foul and temperamental at Christmas when they'd had such a loving start? She knew she probably wasn't the only woman who'd replied to his ad. Was he seeing someone else? Maybe he was looking for someone easier, someone more compatible. Did he think he could do better? Maybe he couldn't bring himself to admit that it wasn't working. Maybe, in spite of all that he'd said, the disability and the wheelchair really were an issue after all.

When she got home the house smelt of René's aftershave, a half empty bottle of wine stood on the table and the ashtray was full of his crushed cigarette ends. She cleared away the breakfast dishes and swept a pile of crumbs off the table.

'Mind Leo!'

She felt crabby and irritable. She'd only known René a few weeks, she should have been able to brush him away as easily as she swept the crumbs off the kitchen table, but his presence lingered. The fact that she couldn't get rid of him only fuelled her annoyance.

'It's over,' she muttered. 'It's OVER.' She lifted a bag of croissants and found a set of house keys tucked underneath—René's house keys. She knew he had a spare set hidden at the side of his house so he wouldn't need them to get in, but he would still need them back at some point. She thought about it for a while and decided to phone him.

'You left your keys,' she said, keeping her voice flat and neutral.

'Yes.' From the tone of his voice René was in no mood to apologise.

'I'll drop them off tomorrow, when I'm passing.'

'Thank you.'

The next day Jane drove to St Nazaire and pulled up outside René's small terraced house. She sounded the horn and René opened the front door seconds later. He must have been watching for her. She wound down the window as he approached the car and silently handed him the keys. René stood by the car, his head bowed, twisting the set of keys around his fingers.

'Jeanne…' He hesitated. 'I don't…I mean…when I…'

Jane took pity on him. 'It's cold René. Why don't you get in the car?'

They went for a drive and René stumbled an apology. 'I've behaved badly, I know, I'm sorry, I can't explain why. I know it was wrong but I couldn't help myself. I don't deserve your friendship, I was foul and you were so kind—

'It's all right René,' Jane said, stopping him mid sentence. 'Christmas isn't an easy time for anyone.' She drove him back to St Nazaire and they agreed to stay in touch.

Word spread that Jane's Christmas with René hadn't gone well and neighbours dropped by to cheer her up. Christine and the children called for tea, Monique came over, Jeannine popped in for a drink and a chat and Francoise brought a huge white cauliflower from her garden. Therese rang to see if Jane needed any shopping done and Jane knew she was fortunate to have found such genuine friends in a close-knit community.

There were things to look forward to. Elise was due to have another baby in a couple of weeks and a friend from England, Louise, was planning to visit. Her daughter Jenny and granddaughter Abby were coming out in March and so was Clive, bearing the long-promised fruit trees.

Life resumed its rhythm. Children came for English lessons and Francoise and Charlotte helped eat the last of the Christmas cake. Angelique took the decorations down and Jane felt relieved to see them go. After such a promising start, Christmas had been a disaster. She was glad to see the back of it.

18 CAUTION

Several days went by and an icy wind blew from the east. It was so cold even the mighty Loire froze over. The camellia tree, normally in full bloom from mid-December, went into hibernation. Its pitifully few buds were clamped shut.

Bijoux broke down again and in desperation Jane took the car to a Rover dealer in Pornichet. It would cost more than the local garage, but maybe they'd do a better job of fixing it. She left Bijoux with them and got a lift home with Francoise.

The gas bottle ran out and Lucien came over to change it. And still there was no word from René. Jane didn't want to be the one to pick up the phone. Her confidence had been knocked by his outburst and she wasn't going to chase him. If he wanted to see her again then he would have to suggest it. Her resolve cracked at the end of the first week in January.

'René? It's Jane.'

'Jeanne! Ca va?' He sounded pleased to hear from her.

'I'm OK. You?'

'No, not so good. I have to go to hospital. They think I have trouble with my heart.' René's voice wavered and he cleared his throat. She wondered if the onset of serious health problems might explain his erratic behaviour and sudden mood swings.

'It's good to hear from you Jeanne,' he said.

'René don't worry if they have to operate. Surgeons are very skilled these days.'

'I hope so.'

He rang back two days later and was especially sweet and friendly. Of all the men she'd met René was by far the most interesting, and the most challenging. Maybe when he came out of hospital they'd be able to resume their relationship? Perhaps it had just been a case of too much, too soon.

Snow poured down, the big freeze continued for another week and without a car Jane was stuck indoors. The phone rang late one afternoon.

'Allo?'

'Madame Lambert?'

'Speaking.'

'Bonjour Madame. This is the Rover garage in Pornichet. Your car, it will need a new oil pump. It will be costly I'm afraid Madame. 4,500 francs. Do you want that we should proceed?'

It was another expense she could ill afford. She rang Clive to see if it would be any cheaper to buy a pump in the UK. 'Sorry Mum, that's about what you'd have to pay here.' Could she survive without a car? No. She'd have to find the money from somewhere. She rang the bank and checked her overdraft—if she went to the limit it would just about cover it. She authorised the repair.

Romain's mum, Maryse, gave her a lift to Pornichet the next day to pick up the car. Jane had never been flush with money but there'd always been just enough to scrape by. Now she was worried.

It was an expensive drive home, starting with petrol. 'Bonjour Madame,' said the garage attendant. 'Cent vingt francs s'il vous plait.' Next stop was the pharmacy for multivitamins. 'Madame Lambert! Ca va? Soixante-neuf francs s'il vous plait.' She bought the basic essentials at the greengrocers, 'Alors quatre-vingt-six francs s'il vous plait Madame.' And she took Fauvette to the vet for her regular contraceptive injection. 'Bonjour Madame. Alors, ca fait cent quatre-vingt-dix francs s'il vous plait. Merci!'

She drove home deep in thought, barely registering Fauvette asleep on the front seat beside her. Could she extend her overdraft? Maybe she could take on more English classes. She was so concerned about finance on the drive back from the vet's surgery that she didn't even notice the sun was out. She got home, opened the car door and Fauvette jumped out.

Jane sat in the driver's seat, waiting for her chair to descend from the roof, watching Fauvette roll in the grass. The air smelt sweet and mild. She looked closer and noticed tiny green shoots pushing their way through the mud. After weeks blanketed in snow and ice the big freeze had finally broken. At last, spring was on its way.

She checked the post box and found a letter from the solicitor in charge of her grandfather's trust fund. It contained a cheque for £750. Yet again Pa Ferdinando had come to her rescue. The distribution of funds from his trust would pay for repairs to the car and put something back in the bank. It was time to celebrate.

There had been occasional calls to and from René while he'd been recovering from an operation and they'd taken cautious steps towards a 'rapprochement.' Now Jane was mobile again, and René out of hospital, it seemed the perfect time for a rendezvous. Whatever had gone wrong over Christmas, she wasn't about to give up. She was willing to accept his behaviour had been a blip caused by ill health.

Neutral territory seemed a good idea. 'Let's go to Monsieur Hulot's beach for a picnic tomorrow,' she suggested. 'If the weather's fine we can walk along the front with Fauvette. If it's bad we can park by the beach and sit inside the car.' René was all for it. 'An excellent idea,' he said. One of the things René admired about Jane was the way she had immersed herself in French culture. Jacques Tati's film, *Les Vacances de Mr Hulot*, was a classic example. When Jane found out it had been shot at St Marc sur Mer, just a few kilometres from St Nazaire, she always referred to that particular beach from then on as 'Monsieur Hulot's beach.'

Saturday 18 January 1997
Get up and make bread pudding, pot tuna and mayonnaise, gin and tonic, flask coffee. Pick up René 11.10am, go to St Marc with Fauvette…thick fog, grey and cloud…

It wasn't the best weather for a picnic but nothing was going to deter Jane. She picked up a fresh baguette on her way to meet René and with a heroic effort at punctuality arrived only ten minutes late. René was already waiting at the front door, wearing a heavy winter coat with a scarf tied around his neck to keep out the cold. They got to the coast just as the morning fog lifted.

René was on his best behaviour, praising the English picnic and playfully flirting with Jane as they promenaded along the front with Fauvette. Shortness of breath soon forced him to sit down and Jane parked her chair next to the bench. Fauvette put her paws on René's knees and he ruffled the fur on her head.

'Alors Fauvette, ca va?' He turned to Jane. 'It's good, sitting here, watching the ocean. Thank you Jeanne.'

Her cheeks flushed. 'My pleasure,' she said.

The thick fog that began the day and the cold skies that ended it did little to spoil their pleasure. They were both in high spirits when it drew time to leave. In spite of the obvious delight they took in each other's company there was no hint from René that he might want to go home with Jane, and she wasn't about to suggest it. She dropped him off in St Nazaire later that afternoon, just as it got dark, and they made no further arrangements to meet. Patience, she counselled herself. Bide your time. He rang the following day.

'It was a fantastic picnic. Thank you, Jeanne.'

Wed 19 February, 1997
Shower and hairwash. I get on bench seat to drain the chair and end up flat on back unable to rise. Jeannine and Eric get me up. Do rest of clothes wash.

Jane spent the morning lying on the bathroom floor. It was a chilly place to lie in mid February, when temperatures had plummeted to a bone numbing three degrees overnight. Even at midday they reached a maximum of just 13 degrees. The electric wall heater clicked off automatically after the first hour and the most Jane could do to feel more comfortable was reach for a towel and drape it over her naked body. It wasn't until Eric arrived for his English lesson, at two o'clock in the afternoon, that she was rescued. Jeannine was called and they went through the now familiar routine of helping Jane back into her chair. The lesson continued as planned.

The calls with René grew more affectionate and three weeks after the picnic it was 'ma chère Jeanne'. Jane decided to risk inviting him to stay the weekend. 'That would be wonderful, thank you Jeanne,' he said.

René arrived clutching a bottle of tequila and several photo albums, showing the holidays he'd been on since his wife had died. The albums were impeccably made up, as neat and orderly as the man himself. Jane tasted her first tequila as she leafed through scrapbooks of Indonesian pictures and souvenirs. René kept and catalogued everything; boarding passes, receipts, foreign currency, postcards, leaflets advertising day trips, ticket stubs. There was even a neatly folded sick bag saved from the aircraft, the corners pinned with precision onto a page of the album.

As an ex Parisian René's default position was superiority over anyone who lived in a rural area. Visitors to Paris often remark on the notorious rudeness of people who live in France's capital city but Parisians disagree. We're not being rude, they say, we're being witty and we like engaging in debate. René was a classic Parisian. Never mind that he hadn't lived in Paris for decades, his inherent sense of superiority ran deep; he'd travelled, he'd worked abroad, what had the local country hicks done?

His sense of superiority was occasionally set aside, such as when Jane's neighbour, Therese, offered to make them 'gallettes' for supper, something Jane wasn't capable of. Whisking eggs was beyond her. The local dish of stuffed pancakes was René's favourite and when Lucien delivered them later that evening, René was full of praise. 'Delicieuse! Fantastique!'

He wasn't so impressed with Jane's cooking.

'I don't like cabbage and I don't like rice,' he declared, staring at his plate. '

Then don't eat it,' said Jane.

The meal may not have been gourmet standard but she knew it was better than anything René cooked for himself. His idea of cooking was to buy a kilo of beans, boil the whole lot in a pressure cooker and live off them for the next fortnight. He regularly burnt the bottom of the pan so when he bought a new batch of beans he bought another pressure cooker and started the whole process again. Jane wasn't too concerned that her cooking might not be what René would have liked. It would have to do. She was beginning to get the measure of him and she realised René was the kind of man she would have to stand up to.

Cooking aside, it was a loving three days. They went shopping together and bought another heater and a coffee pot—both essential for René to feel comfortable at Jane's place. The weather changed that weekend too. The camellia bloomed, the purple crocuses came out and the first daffodils unfurled their cheerful yellow heads. Jane drove René home after the weekend together and he rang the following day, full of tender endearments.

'My little redhead. Ma chère Jeanne. Thank you for all that you did. Let's meet again soon. A picnic. My treat.'

On the first fine Sunday in March, they drove to Saint-Brevin-les-Pins. A busy tourist spot in summer, Saint-Brevin was a sleepy, quiet spot out of season. René may not have been able to cook, but he knew how to shop. He bought a bottle of Bordeaux, slices of cold pork, cold ham, raisin brioche and apples and they drove to a local megalithic site, hidden amongst trees at the edge of a residential area.

Like naughty children they studiously ignored the 'pas de picnic' signs and unpacked their feast in a small clearing by a wooden bench, surrounded by towering prehistoric standing stones. Jane pulled her wheelchair up to the bench and they scoffed their picnic in the warm sunshine, laughing, joking and flirting.

It was a relaxed, easy afternoon and Jane didn't want it to end. As they packed up the illicit picnic she tried to persuade René to come home with her. The suggestion made him clam up. It seemed he didn't want to take their relationship any further. Was he seeing other people? She had no way of knowing. All she knew was that that his 'take it or leave it' attitude was deeply frustrating but she was not about to give up. She dropped him off in St Nazaire and they made no further arrangements to meet.

Thoughts of René were banished when Jane's daughters, Annabel and Jenny, came for a visit in mid March. They marvelled at the back garden, where the field was rapidly being colonised by plants. The daffodils were blooming, the evergreen alyssum saxatile had turned a rich golden yellow and all four peach trees planted the previous autumn—a gift from the builder—had made it through winter. Speckled yellow butterflies, their wings bathed in bright sunshine, flitted through the garden.

Jane invited Elise, Jean Yves, their son Jimmy and their new baby to join them for dinner. They feasted on a 'Jane special'—a mix of English, North African and French dishes, spicy Moroccan sausages served with rice and mixed vegetables followed by bread pudding and biscuits, washed down with Cotes du Marmandais and champagne. Surrounded by family and friends, replete and relaxed, Jane reminded herself that sunshine, friends and pleasurable activities would always keep depression at bay.

Towards the end of the evening René rang. Jane's eyes sparkled when she spoke to him and her voice softened. She was still smiling when she came off the phone and the effect wasn't lost on Jenny.

'Go careful Mum. You know what a miserable time you had at Christmas.'

'It's all right, I know what I'm doing.'

Before they left Jane took her daughters on a tour of the marshland around La Brière. They drove in warm sunshine past the Dolmen du Riholo, the site of an eerie megalithic burial chamber just outside Guérande, where the stones are tumbled in a heap under the trees and overgrown with weeds. They drove to Carnac, on the south coast of Brittany, to marvel at the largest collection of standing stones anywhere in the world—more than three thousand of them hewn from local rock and marching across the fields in long straight lines. Was it some form of early worship? Signs of the Zodiac? Or, as local legend has it, a Roman legion turned to stone by King Arthur? Whatever the answer, the stones fascinated Jane. They drove home in high spirits for a game of Scrabble and an early night.

Jane got up early the next day, while it was still dark, to see her daughters off. They had a long drive ahead of them and they wanted to get going early. Annabel hugged her mum goodbye. 'If it's meant to be, it will be,' she whispered. Jane nodded. She knew what Annabel meant.

19 LOSS

Jane stretched her arms across the examination table, trying to keep the struggling, squirming Leo under control. The vet gently felt along Leo's skinny back leg.

'Is it broken?'

'No, not this time.'

Leo yowled as the vet manipulated his dislocated leg back into place then bandaged it securely. Jane stroked Leo's small head and the little black and white cat nuzzled against her.

'He will be fine. Be sure to keep him inside and give him one of these tablets twice a day.'

'Thank you.'

'A la prochaine fois!' said the cheery vet.

The vet had seen a lot of Jane and her pets; they'd been taking it in turns. First Leo suffered a persistent angry spot on his back where a tick had been removed then Fauvette developed mysterious stomach pains that made her vomit and cry with pain. Two days ago Leo ran off and reappeared with a dislocated back leg. The inconvenience and cost weren't an issue; Leo and Fauvette were part of the family.

Jane took the accident-prone cat home and settled him on a cushion in the kitchen. Inside the veranda she found an old piece of cardboard and leant forwards in her chair to block the cat flap. Leo left his cushion and nosed under her chair to see what she was doing. Jane shooed the curious cat away. He retaliated by sinking his teeth into her hand and Jane flinched and drew back.

In an instant Leo had pushed his way past the cardboard, head butted the cat flap and scrambled through. It clattered shut behind his flickering tail and she watched a ball of black fur leap over the flowerbeds. 'Leo! LEO!' With one last bound and a flash of white Leo disappeared into the long grass.

Several hours later Leo still hadn't come back and Jeanine, Francoise and Lucien all offered to help look for him. Christine, who eked out a precarious existence in two caravans with her gypsy partner, four children, four dogs, a goat, a pony and a clutch of hens, heard what happened and joined the search. She understood the depth of Jane's concern for the missing Leo.

Jane put out food and water, hoping Leo would simply reappear the next day and when he failed to turn up the whole village was alerted to look for him. Leo's leg wasn't broken but without antibiotics there was a danger infection could set in.

Three days passed, then five, then seven and still there was no sign of the missing cat. Jane spent hours pushing her wheelchair along the country lanes, searching and calling his name. She loved the feisty little Leo, could still remember the first day he'd been placed in her cupped hands, and she hated to think he might be suffering. She'd almost given up hope when, on the evening of the ninth day, there was a knock on the back door, just after it grew dark.

'Madame Lambert, I think I have found Leo,' said Paulette, a distant neighbour in the village.

'Thank goodness! Where?'

'In our hay barn.'

'Is he all right?'

'I do not know Madame.' Paulette shrugged. 'We cannot reach him. We have left open the door.'

Jane tried to hide her annoyance. Why hadn't they looked in the barn earlier? Leo could have been trapped there the whole time. If that was the case, he might not have had anything to eat or drink for over a week and he was as skinny as a pipe cleaner as it was. There was no telling how well his leg had healed. It was dark and too late for Jane to go over. She knew she would have to wait until morning.

'Thank you for coming to let me know,' she said. 'Please could you make sure the door stays open and put down food and water? I'll come and get him first thing in the morning.' Before she went to bed, Jane left a bowl of cat food and water in the kitchen, just in case Leo managed to make his way home.

In the middle of the night she heard the cat flap swing open and she recognised Leo's plaintive yowl. 'Viens ici Leo, come here.' She heard him creep into the bedroom and waited to feel his weight land on the end of the bed. Instead Leo curled up on a mat on the floor. She did her best to soothe him with her voice.

'Pauvre petit. Ca va. It's all right. Ne t'inquiet pas mon brave, don't worry my brave little boy.'

In the morning it was clear Leo had used the last of his strength to make it home. He lay on the mat, unable to move. His breathing was fast and shallow, and his leg was swollen and badly infected. It smelt rotten. Jane dressed hurriedly and took Leo straight to the vet.

'Madame Lambert and Leo. Alors, we see you again!'

As the vet examined Leo, his cheerful expression changed. 'Little Leo…' He shook his head. 'I am so sorry Madame. The infection has spread. Leo has gangrene.' He looked at Jane with compassion. 'There is nothing we can do to help him Madame Lambert, it is too late.' Jane cradled the skinny cat in her arms as the vet administered a final pain killing injection.

She drove home in tears, ignoring the roadside flowers that normally gave her such pleasure. In her own garden the cherry tree had blossomed, red tulips were out and daffodils were still in bloom. Tomato seedlings had flourished in the veranda and they would need to be potted up, there were beans to be planted too. She had no appetite for any of it. She knew there was no point moping, keeping busy was the only way to take her mind off Leo, but her heart ached. She couldn't help thinking Leo had suffered and died unnecessarily.

Easter brought a visitor, Jane's good friend Barbara. She was alone this time, having split up with the troublesome boyfriend and the tables were turned. Jane found herself confiding in Barbara, confessing her concern about René—his health worries, his erratic behaviour and his reluctance to commit. Barbara had already heard most of it by phone and she'd consoled Jane many times when René's behaviour had reduced her to tears. She wasn't impressed now.

'You and I both know that men are overrated,' she said sternly. Jane nodded. It was what she had thought when Barbara arrived with her boyfriend, but that didn't make it any easier to hear.

'Do you fancy a trip to St Nazaire market?' she asked.

'You know me,' said Barbara. 'I'm happy to go anywhere.'

'There's something I want to drop off at René's,' said Jane. 'We can do it at the same time.'

They drove to St Nazaire and parked on the street outside René's slender terrace. Jane handed the parcel to Barbara. 'Will you go in? The steps are difficult.' Barbara looked uneasy. 'Does he speak English?

'No, but your French is ok. You'll be fine.'

Barbara took the parcel and knocked on the narrow front door. When René answered she went to hand over the parcel but René motioned her inside. She looked back at the car and Jane nodded, smiling encouragement. 'Go on in,' she called. 'I'm happy to wait out here.'

René's house was exceptionally clean and tidy. Mexican hats were lined up with exact precision on the walls, ornaments stood in neat rows on the shelves and there was a framed photo of his wedding day on the sideboard. René was proud of his mementos and souvenirs and he reached for one of his many photo albums and motioned for Barbara to sit down.

Rene took his time, leafing through photographs and souvenirs of Tibet, and Barbara grew increasingly uncomfortable. Jane was waiting outside and René didn't seem to care. Eventually she got up.

'Well René, Jane is waiting in the car. I have to go.' Reluctantly

René closed the album and showed her to the door.

'Eh bien, au revoir,' he said, and waved to Jane from the doorway.

'How did you get on?' Jane asked.

'Jane, we drove twenty kilometres to deliver a parcel to that man and he couldn't even be bothered to come out and say hello to you!'

'He gets arthritis in his knees,' said Jane. She was prepared to hide her disappointment and excuse René's behaviour but Barbara wasn't. Her opposition to René didn't waver from that point on.

Barbara left and Jane turned her attention to gardening. Late spring had brought the garden to life. Leaves unfurled on the willow tree, sweet peas began their rapid climb and purple iris bloomed above a carpet of dark green ajuga. Jane planted out tomatoes and Lucien put in gooseberries and red currant bushes. She planted gladioli for height and colour, drought tolerant thyme for culinary use and iberis for rapid ground cover. Purple stocks bloomed, spinach thrived and, at the end of April, the old rose planted near la petite cabine—Madame Dieu Donnée—put on a magnificent display of bright red blooms.

Late one Sunday afternoon in early May—a warm sunny day with a soft breeze, perfect gardening weather—Jane was bending over a patch of weeds when she heard someone call her name.

'Madame Lambert!'

She gripped the arm of her chair, lifted herself into a sitting position and raised her head. Shading her eyes she squinted at the figure standing by the gate. It was sixteen-year-old Eric, her star English pupil. She checked her watch. He'd arrived early for his weekly lesson. She dropped her fork and pushed through the long grass towards him.

'J'ai un cadeau,' he said, clutching a cardboard box.

'In English, please Eric.'

'A gift Madame Lambert. I have a gift for you,' he said, handing her the box. Jane reached inside and lifted out a featherweight bundle of grey and white. Eyes the colour of faded bluebells turned to her and Eric rushed to explain. 'Vous n'êtes pas obligé… I mean, you do not have to keep him Madame, but I thought, because you miss Leo…'

Jane smiled. 'He's beautiful. Thank you Eric.'

Fauvette gave the new member of the family her lick of approval and Jane called her new kitten Pablo.

Summer approached and marigold seeds germinated. Tender seedlings pushed their heads above ground, only to have their efforts thwarted by Pablo's sharp teeth and miniature claws.

René was never far from Jane's thoughts. Depending on their last conversation he was either an impossible man—arrogant, self centred, insecure, argumentative and selfish—or the sexiest, most engaging man she'd met in years. Whatever the truth, there was no denying his presence and energy. There were echoes of Richard Burton in *Look Back in Anger*, the charismatic alpha male character, who can't stop picking a fight.

'Come for lunch on Sunday,' Jane said, breaking her resolve not to call. 'I'll pick you up.'

She went all out to impress with a lavish spread of shucked oysters, fresh bread, crisp green salad and chilled white wine. It blew her meagre budget for the week but it had the desired effect. 'Fantastique! Formidable Jeanne!'

Attempts to seduce René later that afternoon weren't so successful. Nothing she did or said would persuade him to stay the night. 'I prefer to go home,' he said primly. Jane drove him to St Nazaire and dropped him off. When she got back to her own house she scribbled on her calendar in teenage-like frustration.

He won't stay. Fuck!

On the face of it, René was in far better shape than Jane. He was tall and solidly built. He had broad shoulders, a wide chest and muscular forearms. His voice was deep and authoritative and his inherent sense of superiority and his commanding presence suggested health and vitality. Jane, on the other hand, was wheelchair bound with limited mobility in her arms and hands. French was a struggle, funds were tight and the house and garden were a long way from being finished.

Yet Jane was far healthier than René, both physically and mentally. René suffered from arthritis in his knees, an as yet undiagnosed heart condition and erratic blood pressure. He was a lonely man with a morbid fear of death. Leaving aside the after-effects of polio, Jane was in good health. Her trump cards were a sunny disposition and positive outlook that convinced her she could overcome any obstacle, including René's resistance. Her sights were set on René and nothing was going to stand in her way.

Two weeks later, fate handed her another opportunity. René had to go into hospital for a minor operation and Jane took full advantage of his captive immobility to press her case. She visited him every day. Her optimism and cheerfulness were in marked contrast to 'Raging Bull' René, forced to examine his own mortality as he lay alone in a dismal hospital bed. Jane was his only visitor. By day four René was well enough to go out for a few hours and Jane drove him to the coast. The sun blazed out of a sky devoid of cloud and as the temperature rose in the car, so did René's temper.

'C'est terminé!'

'Adieu!'

'Adieu!'

He rang the next day to apologise. 'I'm coming out of hospital next week. Maybe we could meet?'

A cynic might have suggested René simply wanted a lift home but Jane saw it as another chance to spend time with him. She collected him from hospital, drove him home and arranged another lunch. There was more champagne, more lavish food and more pressure to stay. The row that ended the lunch was a big one and truths were said on both sides. Jane vowed never to contact him again.

Two days later he rang, full of contrition. 'Jeanne? Ca va?' René was no more willing to give up on the relationship than she was. They arranged to spend the weekend together on the understanding that, whatever else was on offer, it wouldn't be sex.

With the pressure off, René was a changed man. Kind and loving, he fashioned a wedge for the kitchen door, fitted a latch on the petite cabine and made a meticulous chart of the vitamins and supplements Jane was taking. Suddenly there were new hooks in the kitchen, the broken switch on the line trimmer was fixed and the wood saw had a permanent place to hang. It was René's way of coping with Jane's haphazard approach to domestic life. A natural Virgo who loved order and discipline, René itched to have Jane tidy up. If she wouldn't do it, he'd have to do it himself.

They swapped stories. Jane told René about her childhood, her children, the polio, the husbands, her teaching career and her eventual move to France. René spoke about his father, a shoemaker interested in quality, not quantity. The encyclopaedia René's father gave him when he was a child was still one of René's most treasured possessions. Born and raised in Paris, René spent his teenage years under German occupation. His father escaped enlistment because of curvature of the spine and his mother was a nurse, specialising in corsetry and support. It seemed disability really was nothing to worry about.

They chatted easily at the dining room table, René with his sleeves rolled back and his muscular forearms resting on the table, a cigarette never far from his hands. The shelf opposite him was crammed with pictures of Jane's children and grandchildren, letters, notes and postcards from them pinned underneath. René's situation couldn't have been more different. His intransigence towards divorce had forced a rift with one of his daughters when her marriage failed, and the row with his son had happened so long ago René was no longer sure what caused it. He missed being part of a family and felt lost without his wife. 'She did everything for me,' he said. 'I adored her.'

The significance of what he said didn't escape Jane. The phrase 'you can't teach an old dog, new tricks' came to mind. René was used to being looked after and, at seventy-six, he wasn't about to change. That didn't worry Jane as much as it might have done other people. She liked the idea of having someone to look after. All her life people had made decisions for her, now she was living the way she wanted to. She was happy to embrace René, and include him in her life, just as long as he didn't try to control her. After two Libran husbands and three Libran headmasters she'd had enough of people bossing her around.

Given René's natural arrogance and sense of superiority that's exactly what he did, and the consequences were inevitable.

'C'est terminé!'

'Adieu!'

'Adieu!'

20 BATTERED AND BRUISED

'Bonjour Jeanne!'

Jane could hear her neighbour calling somewhere in the distance. Fauvette started barking and there was the sound of claws scratching on glass. From where she lay on the bathroom floor Jane couldn't see anything but she assumed Jeannine was standing outside the back door.

Jeannine! Dans la sale de bain! I'm in the bathroom!

Jane's voice was too faint for Jeannine to hear and Fauvette's barking intensified as the wind rattled the veranda roof. Jane had left the back door unlocked—as usual—so it was only a matter of time before Jeannine let herself in. Eventually there was the sound of the back door being opened.

'Allo? Jeanne?'

'Dans la sale de bain!'

Jeannine crossed the veranda and opened the bathroom door to find Jane lying where she had fallen, her body wedged between the toilet and the washbasin. Jeannine rushed in and knelt down beside her. 'Mais que'est ce que c'est que ca! What happened?' Jane smiled at the look of horror on her friend's face. 'It's so annoying. I fell off the loo. It was a stupid thing to do.'

'Are you hurt?'

'No, I don't think so. Just a bit bruised that's all.' The skin on one side of Jane's face, from above her left eyebrow down to her chin, had started to turn purple and a large lump was visible on her forehead.

'We must call the pompiers! Il faut absolument!'

'No, we don't need the fire brigade. I think if you could just lift under my arms…'

'Mais non! What if you have broken something?'

'I haven't, don't worry. That's it, if you just pick up—ow!'

'Ah non, non, non! Ca vas pas! We must call for help!'

'No really, it's OK, keep going, you're doing well, try and move my legs.'

Jeannine did her best but Jane was too heavy. The angle of her body, trapped as she was between the loo and the sink, made it impossible for Jeannine to lift her back into her wheelchair. There was no option but to call the fire brigade.

Jeannine made the call, came back into the bathroom and manoeuvred Jane into a more comfortable position. She sat sideways on the toilet seat and put her legs behind Jane's back to relieve some of the pressure on her spine. Fauvette joined them, flopping down on the tiled bathroom floor. Jeannine gently combed her fingers through her friend's hair as they sat and waited for the firemen to arrive. The women had developed a close bond since Jane's arrival in the village and there wasn't much they hid from each other. Jeannine knew better than most how Jane could sometimes struggle with daily life.

'Ca va Jeanne?'

'Oh oui, ca va, in fact I'm rich,' Jane said.

'Why, did you win Loto?'

'No. I'm rich because I'm warm, I've got good friends and I've got a place to live without a mortgage.'

Jeannine threw back her head and laughed. 'But Jane, you are also lying on the floor in the bathroom in your nightgown.' Jane's eyes took on a familiar twinkle. 'I know,' she said, 'and with any luck a handsome young fireman is on his way to rescue me right now!'

Four months after he arrived 'Pablo' gave birth to Piplet, Penny, Pierrot, Panthere and Pepin le Bref (King of the Francs and father of Charlemagne). Jane couldn't help thinking she should have inspected

Eric's gift a little closer before accepting it. She sighed at the thought of the work involved over the next six weeks, including the time-consuming search for new owners. She thought about calling René to tell him about the new arrivals but their last meeting had ended with an all too familiar row and she hadn't spoken to him for a while. She decided against it. She was getting sick of his erratic mood swings. One day he'd be sweet and loving, the next he'd lose his temper at the slightest provocation. He'd call in a couple of days and be full of apologies but right now she didn't want to speak to him. She'd had enough.

After a week of silence Jane began to waver. René had never left it this long before. It was down to him to apologise, they both knew that, and he always did eventually but maybe she should give him the opportunity. She rang his home number and got no reply. When there was no answer the next day, or the day after, she began to worry

'René hasn't rung and I can't reach him,' she confided to guests, who were visiting from England. 'I'm worried something's wrong.' Her guests had heard all about the on again, off again relationship with René and their sympathy was limited.

'Maybe he's had enough?'

'That would make two of us!' she declared defiantly, secretly hoping that wasn't true.

She called Barbara in the UK. 'I'm worried about René,' she said.

'Why?'

'We had a row. He hasn't called and he's not answering the phone. It's been over a week now.'

'Oh for heaven's sake you sound like a schoolgirl with a crush.'

Jeannine was the only one who took Jane's concerns seriously. 'What do you think has happened?' she asked.

'I don't know. He may have had a fall. His heart hasn't been too good lately.'

'Do you want me to check the hospitals?'

Jane took a deep breath. 'Yes. Yes please. Will you try the cardiac wards?'

Jeannine rang St Nazaire Hospital and explained in rapid French who she was looking for. 'Un moment. Ne quittez pas,' said the voice on the other end. Jeannine put her hand over the mouthpiece. 'They're checking,' she whispered.

The bubble of worry Jane had nursed all week filled her stomach with cold, empty space. She had a feeling it would be bad news and her instincts were rarely wrong. It took several minutes before anyone came back to the phone.

'Allo? Yes, Mr Dard is here. He is in cardiac intensive care.' Jeannine looked at Jane and nodded confirmation.

'Will you ask if he's all right,' said Jane. Jeannine relayed the question to the nurse on the other end of the phone. 'You are family?' the nurse asked.

'No, I am calling on behalf of a close friend.'

'Alors, I can tell you that Mr Dard is out of danger, but he is still very ill.'

Jeanine passed the message on to Jane. 'Will you ask her if I can speak to him?' Jeanine posed the question, nodded at the answer and handed the phone to Jane. She waited to be connected, her heart thudding faster than normal.

'Allo?' René's normally booming voice was hesitant.

'René? C'est Jane.'

'Jeanne…ma Jeanne. It's good to hear your voice,' he said.

'It's good to hear yours, too.'

'How long have you been in hospital?'

'A few days.'

'Can I come and see you?'

'Si tu veux—if you want to.'

Jane left the visitors and kittens to fend for themselves and drove straight to St Nazaire hospital. She parked, released her chair from its overhead box and waited impatiently for the hoist to inch its way down. A porter directed her down the tiled corridor towards intensive care, where she was forced to wait again outside the darkened room while a nurse checked on a figure lying in bed in the far corner. The only sounds were the rhythmic soft beeps of life support machines, the hushed murmur of lowered voices and the soft squeak of rubber-soled shoes.

Eventually the nurse came back. 'You may go in Madame, but please do not stay long.'

Jane wheeled towards René's bed, smiling encouragement as she approached. René wept to see her, the tears running freely down his cheeks.

The qualities Jane admired in René—his Parisian sense of superiority, his wit, intelligence, sex appeal and sense of humour—were all great fun and deeply attractive, but they hadn't made her fall in love with him. It was only when Jane saw René hooked up to a heart monitor, a tangle of wires and drips radiating out from his body, that she felt something stronger and more permanent than lust or passion. She saw a proud man lying alone with a mountain of fears and she recognised the frailty, insecurity and hidden vulnerability of a fellow human being. It marked the start of a permanent and lasting love for him.

In between hospital visits Jane found homes for Piplet, Penny, Panthere and Pepin-le-bref. The last kitten—Pierrot—had been destined for an elderly lady who became increasingly infirm and who reluctantly decided she couldn't take him. By 13 weeks Pierrot had established his territory so Jane decided to keep him, adding to her growing menagerie.

Not much gardening was done in between visitors, kittens and trips to hospital, and the weeds fought back. Then the wettest June in history only made up for the coldest, driest winter, leaving no rain for July, August and September. The ground was like concrete and the pond little more than a puddle. Jane consoled herself with the thought that there was always next year.

The spell in hospital softened René and when he recovered he took to spending occasional weekends at Jane's house. He was still a difficult, cantankerous, egocentric ex-Parisian but he was also good company. They played Scrabble, watched films and debated history, science, language, religion and politics. Jane introduced René to opera, musical theatre and choral work by Handel, Bach and Vaughan Williams. Leonard Bernstein's Chichester Psalms in Hebrew could move him to tears.

The rows and bust ups continued of course, and they were equally capable of breaking up on the phone or in person. Theirs was a tempestuous, passionate love affair marked by fiery rows and a clash of tempers. Shut up in measureless content? Not remotely.

'How's it going with René?' I asked during a phone call to Jane.

'I'm glad I met him later in life,' she replied. 'I wouldn't have been ready for him any earlier.'

René suffered another heart attack in October and Jane was by his side as soon as she heard. When he recovered she picked him up from hospital, drove him home to St Nazaire and slipped a recording of love songs inside his bag.

In early December Jane received a call at home.

'Madame Lambert?'

'Oui.'

'This is the hospital at St Nazaire. Monsieur Dard gave us your name and number. He had a fall.'

René had fainted in the street and he was in intensive care again. Jane took him food, books, magazines and music and she drove him home when he was discharged. Christmas was fast approaching.

'We could spend it together,' Jane suggested, tactfully not mentioning the disaster of the year before.

'Yes,' said René. 'I'd like that.'

Jeannine called in for a cup of tea one frosty afternoon in mid-December. 'Alors, what about Christmas,' she asked. 'Do you have any visitors this year?'

'René is coming to stay.'

Jeannine raised her eyebrows. She had seen Jane shed bitter tears over the elusive René and she hadn't forgotten the disaster of last Christmas, even if Jane seemed to have put it behind her.

'Are you sure?' she asked.

'It's OK, tout va bien,' Jane replied.

Snow blanketed the garden when Jane collected René on Christmas Eve and more was forecast. On the way back to Maca they stopped at a supermarket to choose food they would both enjoy. They were on their best behaviour, neither wanting a repeat of the previous year. If it went wrong this year they both knew it would mark the end of their relationship.

The wind plucked at their clothes as they unloaded the car, stinging their faces with needles of snow as it swirled mounds of powdery crystals into shifting piles at the back door. Inside though, it was warm and draught-free.

Jane had used her grandfather's money for a proper roof on the veranda and the heavy metal door with its wonky lock that froze in winter had gone too. In its place was a well-insulated plastic door that kept the heat in and the cold out. An unexpected refund from the UK tax office helped pay for the installation of night storage heaters, which meant the house was warm in the morning and stayed that way all day.

As temperatures dipped and frost hardened the ground outside, Jane and René were snug and cosy inside. Fairy lights sparkled on a miniature Christmas tree, dozens of cards lined the walls and Fauvette greeted René like a long lost friend, wagging her tail with enthusiasm.

That night they feasted on trout and rich pate, a thoughtful gift from Jeannine that saved Jane having to cook, and on Christmas Day Jane served an easy casserole of coq au vin, with plenty of vin. Jeannine and Robert called in to wish them 'Joyeux Noel', as did Francoise, Benjamin, Charlotte and Jean Yves.

It would have been a miracle if they had managed to get through Christmas without a row, but at least it was just the one. Jane made an insensitive joke about sex on Boxing Day and René erupted. Knowing the consequences they quickly made up and were friends again by nightfall.

Late winter snow fell silently at the window as a mass of camellia blooms unfurled their petals above the whitened grass. Crocuses punctured the crisp white surface with a vivid splash of purple and when the snow and frost started to melt the glossy leaves of a spreading periwinkle appeared, soon to be covered in a mass of blue star-like flowers. Even a tiny pansy popped out.

'Jeanne,' said René.

'Oui?'

'Merci pour… merci, ma Jeanne.'

They toasted the New Year with champagne. As far Jane was concerned René was now 'my René'.

21 LOYALTY AND LOVE

While Jane was quietly pursuing her goal of finding a French lover—replying to ads with good humour and approaching each blind date with optimism—I was on a race for the finish line. Desperate to shake off my single status, I embarked on a round of speed dating, failing to see the fun in any of it.

We were like the hare and the tortoise in Aesop's Fable. I was racing ahead and Jane was ambling along, enjoying the journey, biding her time and creating her new life. She was confident that when the time was right, she would find what she was looking for.

My own search for a partner was frenetic. In my late 30s by now, I was convinced time was running out. When speed dating didn't work I tried the internet and lied about my age, using an old photograph to reinforce the lie. I never once thought what might happen if any of the available men actually wanted to meet me.

On a rare date I came clean and admitted I was closer to forty than I was to thirty. 'If you can lie about that, you can lie about anything,' said the attractive young man sitting opposite. He was right. I could and did lie about many things in the hope it would get me a man.

At various times I feigned an interest in classical music, clog dancing, folk music and sailing, all in the vain hope it would lead to matrimony. I was so far behind my friends, nearly all of them married with children (some greedily onto their second go) that drastic action was called for. I felt compelled to cut to the chase and get married before it was too late.

While Jane was demonstrating her love and loyalty towards Rene, I was leap frogging my way towards the ideal husband, or so I hoped. On a brief holiday to Australia I met someone I thought was perfect.

Alex had a steady job, a regular income, two young children and a wife who had just left him. It was an ideal, ready-made family I could step into and save the bother of having to create one of my own. I cast myself in the role of caring potential stepmother and loving new partner, willing to make whatever sacrifice was necessary in order to stand by the grieving, wronged man she loved. It was easy to convince myself I'd fallen in love. I set out to woo Alex long distance, convinced we were meant for each other. It was a foolish plan, doomed to fail.

In summer 1998 I arrived at Jane's house with the elusive Australian in tow. I probably looked a lot like Barbara, when she arrived with her boyfriend. I had been flitting back and for between England and Australia, spending up to three months at a time in Sydney, where I used up most of my dwindling savings chasing an elusive dream of love.

In spite of my best efforts Alex was still pining for his ex-wife and unwilling to commit to a relationship with me. I ignored the stilted conversations that left me baffled and I tried soothing his broken heart. I figured the nicer I was the more likely he'd be to fall for me. After numerous trips to Australia I had finally persuaded him to make the journey over to England. We were on a week's holiday in France, staying one night with Jane.

Jane was as sunny, colourful and good humoured as ever, although she looked tired. The house had improved since I'd seen it last and it now had heating and new roofs. The grain store had been decorated and the garden had the beginnings of shape and structure. A concrete path wound its way around the entire plot and a central line of pavers bisected it. There was a mini orchard of fledgling apple and peach trees to one side, and a pond with a graceful weeping willow and an abundantly fruitful young damson tree on the other side. Much of the bare earth was hidden under a mix of herbs, vegetables, shrubs, bulbs, roses and flowers. I spotted white, purple and yellow gladioli, runner beans, broad beans, marrows, potatoes, tomatoes, geranium—and a lot of weeds. Alex and I spent a couple of hours weeding while Jane went to fetch René.

We were still weeding when René arrived. I watched a tall man, dressed in grey slacks, short sleeved brown shirt and blue braces unfold himself from Jane's car. He approached across the garden, a little unsteady on his feet but full of alpha male charisma, and he shook hands with Alex then he grabbed me by the shoulders and kissed me on both cheeks.

'You are friends of Jane? Then you are also my friends!' he declared. 'Come and have a drink with me!'

We went inside and René motioned for us to sit down.

'Perhaps we should give Jane a hand preparing lunch,' I suggested.

'Mais non!' said René, 'you must sit and talk to me.'

I looked across at Jane who was rummaging in the fridge. 'Jane, can we give you a hand?'

She lifted her head and smiled. 'No thanks, you sit and talk to René.'

René opened a bottle of wine, poured us each a glass then lit a Gauloise cigarette. He had the solid build of a rugby player and I thought of that children's cartoon character, Desperate Dan, with his square jaw and large, unshaven chin. René pulled on the cigarette cupped between his huge fingers, blew out a plume of smoke and bombarded us with questions. Since he spoke no English and Alex spoke no French I was forced to translate.

'You are from Australia, how far is that? How long was your flight? Here, have another glass of wine. Do you smoke? Have a cigarette. I can speak English. Good morrnink; good afterrrnoon; my taylorr is reech; ze book is on ze table.' As the wine flowed René's personality expanded and I was hard pressed to keep up with the barrage of questions.

'What is it like in your country? Will you send me a postcard from

Australia? Here, have another glass of wine.'

He reached down to stroke Fauvette, who was sitting at his feet, staring up at him, waiting for scraps to fall. 'She loves me. Don't you Fauvette?' René lifted his head, beaming with pride. 'Jane has many friends. They all love her. And now they all love me too. Jane's friends are my friends,' he declared, waving his cigarette and spilling ash on the table. 'Jane's home is my home. Isn't that right Jane?'

Jane shot an ironic glance at me and smiled indulgently at René. 'That's right René,' she laughed.

There was something naive and touching in the way René had signed his own adoption papers, admitting him to the loyal circle of Jane's many friends and family. In typically generous fashion Jane was including René on occasions she thought he'd enjoy. It was clear that a man as gregarious as René would have found it hard to be alone. Jane had told me that René was never far from slipping into depression and she knew the remedy—good company.

'Is this your boyfriend?' René asked.

'Yes,' I said, crossing my fingers under the table. Rene leant forward across the table and tapped me on the hand. 'Do not let him know that you love him,' he said, looking directly at me. Too late, I thought, choosing not to translate that particular comment.

I could see the attraction of René's charismatic personality and Jane clearly adored him but, like so many others, I thought René was a lot of work. His entrenched male position made him unwilling to help around the house, and that made things difficult for Jane. I wondered if that explained why she looked so tired.

While Jane was driving René home after lunch her next-door neighbour Jeanine popped in and she didn't hesitate to air her views. 'René just sits there, there's a sink full of dirty dishes, and he doesn't lift a finger to help,' she said. 'Jane's exhausted. Surely he can see that. What's wrong with the man?' Initially so encouraging when Jane embarked on her search for a lover, Jeannine was now increasingly concerned that René was too much for her.

Any new partner faces scrutiny from friends and family, and it was a measure of how much people cared for Jane that they got so worked up about her choice of partner. There was also a hint of possessiveness in that concern. René was a potential threat to the close friendship some people had with Jane. And how much was it to do with Jane's disability? Would any of us have been so quick to criticise René's lack of support if Jane hadn't been in a wheelchair?

The main complaint against René was that he exhausted Jane, that he sat back and allowed her to do everything without lifting a finger to help. That's not an uncommon complaint for any couple. The argument most people used against him was that René wore Jane out, but if Jane had listened to that kind of argument in the past, she never would have succeeded in getting her children out of care. Well-meaning social workers were all too ready to say. 'It will be too much for you.' Jane stubbornly ignored them. Now she was facing a similar onslaught of concern and she was determined to resist any suggestion that she dump René. Jane may have been disabled but there was nothing disabled about her will. She wanted to look after René. She loved him.

No doubt some people would have preferred Jane to find a polite, mild mannered kindly old man to enjoy her retirement with. René was anything but. He was an alpha male with arrogant Parisian principles. He thought most country people were provincial hicks and he took no pains to hide his opinions. The detractors who thought René was muscling in on Jane and taking advantage of her good nature saw him as an opportunist, looking for free board and lodging. In fact it was Jane who kept encouraging René to stay over, and René who resisted.

When she left England, Jane made it clear she wanted independence. The move to France gave her the control she craved and she was finally living life on her own terms, no matter now imperfectly or with what difficulty, she was living it. Why then, why was it so hard to accept that she should control her choice of partner?

In my case I wondered where the romance was. I'd been fed a diet of fairy stories in childhood and I gulped down a glut of historical romances as a teenager. I expected love to be romantic. I looked for flowers and chocolates, sweet gestures, tender moments. When I didn't find them I invariably gave up and sulked in a corner.

Love for Jane was far more practical. She had a gutsy determination to face reality and, far from expecting René to behave like a fictional romantic lover, Jane accepted him for what and who he was. She loved his arrogant charm, his wit and his intellect. He was the most challenging, exhilarating company and he lifted her spirits in a way no one else could. There were times René made her feel like a giddy teenager, other times she could cheerfully have throttled him. There was no doubt she loved him. The question was, did René feel the same way?

The answer came at breakfast one morning. Jane was enjoying her morning cup of tea with toast and English marmalade and René was sitting opposite in his shirtsleeves, dipping slices of baguette, liberally spread with butter, into a large cup of milky coffee. Fauvette was under the table, scratching, licking and occasionally squealing.

'She is ill, no?' said René, reaching down to pat her.

Jane shook her head. 'It might be fleas,' she said, and took a generous bite of toast.

'You think?' said René.

Fauvette knew she was being talked about. She placed a paw on René's knee and looked trustingly up at him. René stroked her head and slipped her a piece of soggy bread.

'Did you enjoy that walk I took you on, hmm?'

'We'll give her a dose of flea treatment later,' said Jane.

After breakfast René held Fauvette steady while Jane broke a capsule of flea treatment and dabbed it between the dog's shoulder blades. René tickled Fauvette through her thick woolly coat.

'She loves me, don't you think Jeanne?'

Jane was far too busy trying to apply the correct dosage to worry about René's fragile ego.

'Yes René, Fauvette loves you.'

'Do you love me Jeanne?'

Jane stopped what she was doing and raised her head. 'René, you irritate me beyond words, but yes, I love you.'

René beamed. 'Moi aussi!' he said.

It was a declaration of sorts, and it would have to do.

Barbara made her annual visit to France in early spring and she and Jane spent five days touring St Marc, Pornichet, La Baule, Le Pouliguen, Batz sur Mer and Le Croisic. They relished the time they had together and renewed the close bond that existed between them, in the way that friends who've known each other for years can do so easily.

Jane made a point of inviting René to stay for the last two days of Barbara's trip, hoping they would get to know each other better, and he arrived clutching his prized photo albums full of souvenirs from trips to India and Tibet. He was keen to show them to Barbara but she was more interested in seeing how he treated her close friend. She couldn't fathom what Jane saw in René and nothing escaped her notice. She simmered with righteous indignation as René sat at the table, waiting to be served a meal and she watched with growing incredulity as he lit another cigarette and helped himself to a glass of wine while Jane was busy in the kitchen.

'I've got your measure,' she muttered.

'Comment?' he said.

Barbara shook her head. 'Nothing René.'

She smiled at him and discreetly moved two bottles of sherry out of his reach. She'd bought them as a gift for Jane and she didn't want him helping himself. 'Damn self-centred is all you are,' she whispered.

In all the years she and Jane had known each other, Jane had always been single. When they met Jane was already a widow, there'd been the occasional lover since but never anyone serious. Now there was a man in Jane's life and it wasn't someone Barbara approved of. What's more, it looked like he was sticking around.

Late one afternoon Barbara and Jane went food shopping, leaving René in front of the television. A self confessed straight talking woman, Barbara wasted no time. 'Jane, does René do anything to help in the house?'

'He doesn't need to.'

'Yes he does! He's making extra work for you and he's doing nothing in return.'

They made their way down the aisle, adding cheese, yoghourt and milk to the trolley. 'What about food? Tell me he is at least contributing to the food bills.' Jane consulted her list and added stewing steak to the trolley.

'Quelque fois,' she said calmly.

Barbara erupted. 'Sometimes! Jane, that's not good enough! René should be making more than just an occasional contribution. You can't afford to support someone else.' She was convinced René was taking advantage and that Jane was blind to his faults.

'I'll manage,' said Jane. 'Besides, you don't know him,' she added. 'He lost a lot of friends in the war.'

It was an argument that held little sway with Barbara. 'What's that got to do with anything?' she retorted.

'It matters,' said Jane, closing the conversation.

They got back to the house and unloaded the shopping while René sat in front of the television.

'Shall I put the kettle on Jane?' Barbara asked.

'I rather fancy something stronger,' said Jane. 'What about opening that sherry?'

Barbara reached for one of the bottles she'd tucked out of reach on the sideboard and pulled the cork. It came out easily, far too easily. She lifted the bottle, felt the weight of it and stalked into the sitting room, waving the half empty bottle in front of René's face. 'You drank it! René, vous avez buvez le sherry!' she yelled. René waved a hand at her and growled something incomprehensible in French. Barbara growled back in English. 'You are *very* greedy René!' Later that day she hid the second bottle upstairs.

As far as Barbara was concerned, René's arrival on the scene was a disaster. She was convinced Jane had lost the ability to think rationally.

22 ACTION!

'Pas de dioxines sur ma tartine!'

Jane's angry shouts were swallowed by the buffeting wind. It whipped her orange hair into a frenzy that rivalled her own passionate pleas. Dressed in trademark green floral shirt, red trousers, blue shoes and her favourite spotted hat, Jane was blocking the bridge that spans the road from Donges to St Nazaire. She wasn't alone. Dozens of industrial tractors parked nearby dwarfed her red wheelchair. A group of cows could be seen ambling about in the background, a snarl of backed-up traffic stretching behind them.

Jane took off her hat and waved it at the television cameras. 'Pas de dioxines sur ma tartine! Keep those dioxins off my toast!'

Thirty tractors, five cows, a group of farmers and a handful of environmentalists had blocked the bridge in protest at plans to build a new incinerator at Donges. There was a suggestion the incinerator would be used to burn plastics, and if that was the case Jane wanted none of it.

She knew that when chlorinated plastic is burnt it produces dioxins, highly toxic chemicals that even at small concentrations can prove lethal to humans and wildlife. Agent Orange, used during the Vietnam War, contained just such a dioxin and Jane was determined not to allow the pristine landscape around La Brière to be contaminated by such a threat.

Four years previously Jane had never even been to France, now she was actively involved in local issues. It was one of the things René admired about Jane—her willingness to participate, to get involved and take action. In Jane's view, if a serious issue was at stake, inactivity wasn't an option.

When it came to relationships, Jane knew nothing could be achieved without a measure of hard work. She realised her relationship with René wouldn't blossom overnight and she was prepared to put up with the pain, willing to wait for the gain.

His regular visits had gradually been extended and now René came to stay most weekends. Francoise would pick him up on Thursday or Friday after she finished work then drop him back in St Nazaire on Monday or Tuesday, which saved Jane having to make the return journey twice a week. As well as listening to music and watching television, she and René amused themselves with reading, Scrabble, crosswords and conversation.

'The French didn't invent croissants, the Chinese did.'

'No they didn't.'

'Yes they did, look it up.'

'I will.'

'Did you know churches in Malta have two clocks? It's so they can confuse the devil; he won't know what time mass is on.'

'Why aren't evil people assassinated? It seems you've got to do something worthwhile to be a good candidate for assassination. Kennedy, Martin Luther King, Indira Ghandi, they were all assassinated. What about Stalin? Hitler? No-one killed them, did they?'

'True,' said René. 'Are you going to bother to vote?'

René asked the seemingly innocent question while he was cleaning his shoes. European elections were being held in a few weeks time and, for the first time since she'd arrived in France, Jane qualified to vote. René couldn't see the point—the turnout for European elections was traditionally low, and who cared about the European Union anyway? Jane wheeled around to face him.

'Am I going to vote? What sort of question is that? Of course I am! Why did Hitler get in? Because people didn't vote, that's why. Women fought for years to be allowed to vote and I'm not about to throw that vote away. The European parliament has proportional representation, which means every vote counts and I'm certainly going to use mine. I suggest you do the same!'

René carried on cleaning his shoes.

Jane read all she could in the local papers, listened to the news, quizzed anyone and everyone she met and decided her allegiance lay with the Ecology Party—Les Verts—led by Franco-German politician Daniel Cohn-Bendit. Les Verts did well, winning almost ten per cent of the vote and capturing nine seats in the European parliament, ahead of the Union for French Democracy, the French Communist Party, the Hunting, Fishing, Nature and Traditions Party and Jean Marie Le Pen's National Front. René's own allegiance was closer to the latter than to the Greens and his slightly alarming racist views didn't go down well with Jane.

Above all, René loved children and animals and Jane was surrounded by plenty of both. She had her gardening gang, her English pupils, her children, grandchildren and now a growing number of great grandchildren. One by one she introduced them all to René. Her huge circle of close friends and family were in constant touch, in marked contrast to René's solitary life. The only member of the family he stayed in touch with was his oldest daughter, Francoise. A nurse with three children, she visited whenever she could from her hometown several hundred kilometres away.

The main obstacle between René and most of Jane's friends was that he didn't speak English and they didn't speak French. That didn't stop him collecting more adoption papers in late October when Annabel and Jenny arrived for a whirlwind visit with Annabel's son, Xavier. By the end of the 24-hour stopover they all loved René and René loved them all. It seemed everyone was happy.

Jane's daughters didn't share the concerns some of her friends and neighbours had about her relationship with René. It was a measure of René's charm that he won them over, to the point where Annabel thought her mum was a bit harsh on him. She thought René seemed a lovely chap.

The arguments between Jane and René lessened but when they did happen they were still deeply upsetting. One night René took things too far.

'I've had enough, I'm leaving first thing in the morning,' he shouted, his face flushed with rage and too much red wine. He looked for something to vent his frustration on and aimed a kick at Jane's wheelchair. His boot struck the wheel and the kick sent a shudder through the frame.

It was too much for Jane. She snatched the keys from the kitchen table. 'No you're not. You're leaving now. Right now!'

René hesitated, it was past midnight and they'd both been drinking.

'I mean it!' she said. 'Get your things!'

Jane didn't bother to wait for a reply and she wheeled out to the car, exasperated by yet another late night row that had erupted out of nowhere. By the time René emerged, clutching his bulging overnight bag, his head lowered like an angry bull, Jane had the engine running. She sat in the driver's seat, watching him shuffle towards the car, quelling any sympathy she knew she could so easily feel for him, and she drove him back to St Nazaire in stony silence.

Over the days that followed she refused to answer his calls and she vented her frustration in a letter. *Men are only good for one thing—and some of them aren't even any good at that,* she wrote.

In the end though, they found that being apart was worse than being together. René was an emotional man, easily upset, and he hated rowing, never mind that he was so often the cause. They made up over lunch at the local supermarket, black flour gallette and beer for René, Coquilles St Jacques and a glass of wine for Jane.

Jane's garden flourished that year, and the newly planted apple trees—Cox, Blenheim and Discovery—came through winter in good shape. Easter brought the first blossoms on the cherry tree and on the twenty-sixth of April, at ten in the morning, Jane heard the sound she'd been waiting for, the first nightingale of spring.

May brought a mini heat wave and Jane was hard pressed to cope with dozens of thriving tomato plants. Eric took six for his mum, Jeanine took another four and Jane planted out the remainder.

June 1999

The good news of the day—I've won the lotto again this time 14 francs! I've blown it on some cherries, which are being eaten in the garden, which is very sunny and hot until the breeze blows up. We love a heat wave Fauvette and I... Work in the garden is tough again. I'm thinking of going for the tallest weed trophy. I've got lots of seedlings and little plants that are screaming to be settled in a patch of their own so I have to clear a patch and plant some out.... My dear little swallows are back in my little cabine, they have built a new nest beside the old one. I'm afraid Pierrot killed one that was on the ground and left the corpse under my bed. Now the others dive-bomb him as he walks past their home... A great disappointment on the wildlife front is the absence of the nightingale. I heard him one night and then no more. Perhaps they don't like fully grown cats or magpies fighting with jays... Our new little neighbours have made up for our disappointment. The old lady Marie, who lives on the other corner of our little side road, has a very large garden, most of which is a cornfield or hayfield, anyway uncultivated, which is not surprising as she is 87. Lucien in the village keeps a few sheep and he brings them into the garden as lawn mowers...

Jane's gardening team—Les Trois Mousquetaires as they had been dubbed—attacked the rising tide of grass after Jane was forced to admit defeat in a two-day battle with the line trimmer.

Old-fashioned sweet peas bloomed against a sunny wall of the petite cabine, their heady perfume mingling with the sweet smell of freshly mown grass. The garden beds, now clearly marked out, bore sturdy gladioli that pushed their thick stems towards the sun, and the few broad beans that had survived the winter frosts followed by an onslaught of slugs, were ready to be harvested.

It barely made a meal but Jane wasn't deterred. She planted runner beans instead and hoped for better things. At least the new damson tree was doing well, it promised a bumper crop later in the year. Swallows were nesting in the petite cabine again, bats were regular visitors and the owl swooped silently past at night, searching for any rats or mice Pierrot might have missed.

Jane made the most of the long daylight hours, weeding, clearing, watering, planting and harvesting. Pumpkin seeds went in, new potatoes and juvenile runner beans came out. With the arrival of really hot weather, the evening primrose burst into bloom and swaying hollyhocks began their majestic ascent, improbable ladders of flower stretching towards the sun.

Dead grass, left to dry after the frenzy of mowing and trimming a few weeks earlier, was dug into the borders where herbs, perennials, bulbs and roses jostled for space. A passion fruit vine sprawled over the wall of the petite cabine and tall thistles, which Jane had stopped her gardening gang from chopping down, were now attracting goldfinches.

The swallow chicks learnt to fly and greenfinches hopped under the new archway, where the twisted tendrils of climbing roses had started their long journey to the top. Throughout it all the gardening gang kept Jane company, occasionally joined by Jeannine, Paulette or Robert, who often volunteered to weed out the front.

Summer slipped by and autumn came and went with a bumper crop of tomatoes that kept Jane busy bottling, chopping, cooking and preserving. The jars were handed out as gifts, small tokens to thank neighbours for their help.

At the first sign of winter the lemon tree was trimmed and brought indoors along with the potted orchid and lemon geranium. Romain cut the grass for the last time in early November, skimmed the pond and put the gardening tools away for winter. Jane scrubbed the big pots and saucers and turned up the heating.

'Bijoux' didn't like the cold weather any more than Jane did. Her old Rover was in and out of the garage several times over summer and with the onset of cold weather Bijoux gradually shut down. First the speedometer went, then a tyre had to be replaced and then the car refused to start. The new battery, fitted only five months earlier, was mysteriously flat.

The garagiste came, towed the car away, checked it and returned it. 'Ca va maintenant,' he said, but it wasn't ok. Two days later Bijoux broke down again, the tow truck came back and Jane's car was carted off.

Ten days later Jane got a call to say her car was ready. 'Please could you have a cheque ready Madame Lambert?' It was an expensive repair.

With Christmas just weeks away, Jane was keen to make plans for when René would be coming. She tried calling him to let him know the car was back on the road but each time she rang, the phone went unanswered. With a sinking feeling she rang the local hospital.

An efficient receptionist answered in rapid French.

'Ici l'hôpital de St Nazaire. Je vous écoute.'

'Ah, bonjour,' said Jane. 'Cardiologie s'il vous plait.'

'Ne quittez pas. Hold the line.'

Jane waited for the call to be put through.

'Allo?'

'Ah bonjour. Je cherche Monsieur René Dard.'

'Ah oui. Monsieur Dard est ici.'

The nurse went on to explain that René had fallen in the market at Saint Nazaire. He wasn't badly hurt but the hospital wanted to keep him in for observation.

Jane went to visit him and he was a sorry sight, his face and hands covered in cuts and bruises and his broken glasses propped on the bedside cabinet. He seemed frail and unsure of himself. 'I fell over, there was a man, a pied noir,' he said.

Jane waited nervously for what might come next. 'Pied noir' was the colloquial term for a French Algerian, a group of immigrants who weren't always welcomed in France. Knowing how wild some of René's views were, Jane hoped he wasn't about to come out with anything offensive.

'He was kind,' said René. 'He helped me. He picked me up and offered to buy me a cup of coffee.' René plucked at the sheet covering his bruised body and Jane put her hand over his.

'I'm glad he helped you René. When will you be able to come out?'

'Tomorrow.'

'I'll come back and fetch you.'

The next fall was more serious. René broke his shoulder and was taken into hospital for surgery, so Jane rang to see how he was. 'Can you tell me what ward Mr Dard is in?' she asked.

'Ca vaux pas la peine,' said the unsympathetic nurse, telling Jane bluntly it wasn't worth visiting. 'He'll be unconscious, we have to operate,' she added.

Jane bristled at the indifferent tone. 'What about when he comes round?' she said. 'Do you have someone to sit by his bed?'

'No.'

'Then that's what I will do.'

Jane drove to the hospital and arrived in time to see René coming out with his arm in a sling, accompanied by a male nurse who stopped to talk to Jane. 'Mr Dard really shouldn't go home alone,' he said. 'He needs someone to look after him. He won't be able to manage on his own.'

Jane nodded. 'Do you want to stay with me René?' she asked. René's eyes shone with unshed tears.

'Oui, s'il te plait.'

He stayed a month to recuperate, and somehow never went home again.

23 WORK REST AND PLAY

'This traffic's terrible, turn right.'

Jane was in the centre of St Nazaire, trapped in a snarl of cars that weren't going anywhere. Traffic was flowing in the opposite direction but there was an obstruction ahead and they hadn't moved for several minutes. René pointed towards a narrow turning on the right.

'There, turn right!'

Jane glanced at the no entry sign. 'I can't, it's a one way street.'

'I go down it all the time.'

'That's when you're on foot. I'm in a car.'

'It won't matter.'

'René, I can't.'

'Turn right!'

'No!'

'Merde alors!'

René wrenched open the passenger door, stepped out and found he was standing in the middle of a stream of traffic. Jane leant across. 'René don't be ridiculous. You'll get run over. Get back in the car!'

René slammed the car door and weaved unsteadily through the oncoming traffic. 'Good luck to you!' Jane shouted at his retreating back.

René could drive but he chose not to. He left that to Jane. For a man with a heart condition he coped surprisingly well with the accidents Jane and Bijoux attracted.

There was the time the manager of the local supermarket reversed his BMW into Bijoux while Jane was stationery in the supermarket car park. Another time a car sped through a stop sign as she and René drove past a T-junction. The speeding driver hit the side of Jane's car and drove off without stopping. 'Are you all right René?' Jane asked, frantically scrabbling for a pen to write down the number plate. 'French country drivers,' René grumbled. 'They don't know the first thing about driving. Paris is the only place they know how to drive.'

Another time René was in the passenger seat when Jane drove past a lorry parked on her side of the road. A car pulled out of a driveway hidden behind the lorry and Jane didn't have time to swerve. There was a glancing blow, followed by the familiar sound of crunching metal and glass.

'Are you all right René?'

'Yes, you?'

'I'm fine but the car has taken a bash. Will you see if the other driver is all right?'

René got out to remonstrate and came back full of sympathy. 'She's only just passed her test. It wasn't her fault, poor thing, she couldn't see, there was a van parked in the way.' It helped that the driver in question was young and pretty.

René wasn't as understanding if the accident was Jane's fault. With the steering wheel on the right Jane was always nearest the verge, which made overtaking a challenge. On the plus side it meant she could look out for wildflowers that flourished on the banks of streams and ditches running beside many of the country lanes around Donges and Maca.

'Is that batchelor's button?'

'I don't know,' said René, keeping his eyes firmly on the road.

'Can you see that little blue carpet of flowers?'

'No.'

'I think they might be—'

'Attention Jeanne!'

With a sudden jolt Jane's front wheel slipped into the ditch. René lit up, erupting into a stream of angry French.

'C'est pas possible! Qu'est ce que tu fais maintenant? Alors, tu n'as jamais—'

'Oh René shut up.' Jane took a deep breath and tried to calm her nerves. They'd already had a row in the supermarket and she couldn't face another one. 'Could you please get out and have a look at the front wheel, maybe I can reverse out.'

'Mais non! Ca va pas. Tu n'auras jamais –

'René will you just have a look?'

René got out, slammed the door and gave a cursory glance at the front wheel then he threw up his arms.

'C'est impossible! Impossible!'

Jane knew she'd get no help from René until he had calmed down. It's just as well you don't drive, she thought, a man of your temperament shouldn't be allowed behind the wheel.

There was a tap at the window and Jane turned to see a woman with dark curly hair standing outside the car. She wound down her window. 'I saw what happened,' said the dark-haired woman. 'I live just opposite. I have a friend. Maybe he can help? He has a tractor.'

Half an hour later Jane and Bijoux were pulled out of the ditch and René was persuaded to get back into the car. There didn't seem to be any damage so they drove home, and a brooding silence built up in the car until René could contain himself no longer. 'I am an intelligent, good-looking man. You should consider yourself a lucky woman, falling on a man like me. Very lucky indeed,' he announced. He gave a short, sharp nod and folded his arms.

René's pompous words hung in the air and Jane wondered what she'd done to deserve such luck. Maybe she should buy a lottery ticket on the way home. She giggled and René glared at her. His furious expression made her laugh out loud.

'What? Why are you laughing? What is so funny?'

Jane laughed harder, wiping away the tears that streamed down her face. Eventually René joined in.

The arrogant alpha male, the 'better than any country bumpkin' ex Parisian, the man whose culture was far superior to anyone else's, finally conceded that maybe, just maybe, he was the lucky one.

Barbara came to visit the following Easter and for a week they all managed to ignore the fact that she and René didn't get on. Barbara and Jane worked in the garden or drove off to explore during the day, and at night Jane's guest found excuses not to sit in the same room as René. Her opposition was fearsome and she simmered with unspoken resentment.

The real fall out came when Jane invited neighbours for an Easter supper. She and Barbara went out to buy provisions, and it didn't escape Barbara's notice that René was slumped in front of the television when they left and was still there when they came back.

The two women unloaded the car, unpacked the bags and got ready for the party, spreading a clean white cloth on the dining room table, putting out glasses, plates, dishes, knives and forks. They loaded the table with a selection of chocolates, cheeses, cold meat, paté, cakes and pastries. In between the dishes they placed small baskets of flowers, tiny Easter eggs and fluffy yellow Easter chicks. Barbara stood back to admire their handiwork and Jane called René to the table.

He shuffled in, sat down, picked up a knife and started helping himself. Seeing the beautiful display destroyed before anyone else had a chance to see it was too much for Barbara. She flew into a rage.

'René, non! It is not time. You must wait for the guests!' René lifted his head and growled, so Barbara growled right back at him. Nothing could shake her belief that René had found what she called 'a gravy train.'

There was no denying René was a difficult man. He could be kind, loving and full of fun one day then selfish, dictatorial and moody the next. Jeannine called in for a cup of tea one morning and found Jane sitting alone in the dining room, René nowhere to be seen.

'Ca va Jeanne?' she asked.

Jane raised her eyes. 'Men. They say you learn something about yourself in every new relationship,' she said, glancing into the sitting room where René was watching television. 'I've learnt I need my solitude. And I don't like being dictated to,' she added.

Jane's next-door neighbour laughed. 'Bravo Jeanne!' she said. She got up, rinsed the cups and kissed Jane on both cheeks.

'Allez, Jeanne, a bientôt. Au revoir René,' she called.

Jane knew she was lucky to have found neighbours who were kind hearted, good humoured, generous and reliable. She valued their friendship, as they did hers. Being part of a close-knit community meant a lot to her, but if Jane wanted rigorous debate, spirited conversation and someone who challenged her opinions, she turned to René.

'What have the English ever done for France?' he asked out of the blue one day.

'Listen cocky, in the last war the English were the only allies you had in the world,' Jane replied.

René was forced to concede the point. 'We don't speak the same language but you've got a good brain,' he said, without any hint of irony. 'I can discuss things with you, better than I can with my French friends.'

As far as René was concerned, his role in life was limited to conversation and consumption. Learning how to make a cup of tea was his only concession to domesticity.

'Verdi, Puccini, Tosca, they are the do-gooders of the world. Madame Butterfly, that is a magnificent opera,' he declared as they sat listening to a recording of La Bohème.

'A dramatic soprano playing a 15 year old Japanese girl stretches the imagination too far for me,' countered Jane.

Occasionally, they agreed. 'Everywhere they go the Americans cause trouble,' said René.

'George Bush is a rotten little squib,' Jane added, furious at another distressing news broadcast from Iraq. 'He's pushing his country down the drain.'

She found a willing ally in René who hadn't forgotten how Americans had arrived in France at the end of World War Two with pre-printed French dollars, hoping to take over the country they had helped to liberate.

'Les Américains!' he scoffed. 'They tried to buy Credit Lyonnais, can you believe it?'

The solution to heated arguments over the television remote control was separate televisions, one for Jane in the dining room, another for René in the sitting room. The solution to Jane's growing supremacy in French Scrabble was simpler.

'You can't have that word, it's not French,' René declared one night.

'That's funny, the Petit Larousse dictionary says it is,' said Jane calmly.

The next time Jane got the scrabble set out René picked through the tiles and mumbled. 'We don't need to keep score. Let's just play for fun and enjoy the game.'

April 2000

Our news—cold, sunny, wet, windy, hail, thunder—at the moment we are having weather! Nevertheless the daffs are doing well and the irises are out and I'm telling the tulips to go slow and save their efforts for Easter when Pam is coming for a week.... René is ticking over, has lost weight and is not a good colour. He eats well when he is here but I've limited his visits to three days. I'm just too tired to do a longer stretch...

René's health deteriorated, the arthritis in his legs grew worse and he had frequent falls. He was a demanding patient. When he was poorly or in pain, Jane was everything God sent. When he was better it was a different story.

Preparing three meals a day, several days a week took its toll on Jane's own health. She was seventy by now and René seventy-six. Jeannine, Francoise and even Lucien couldn't help notice that Jane's skin had lost its usual lustre, she didn't smile as much and the sparkle in her blue eyes had dimmed. Jeannine longed to help, but what could be done with René there?

Jane felt worse and made an appointment to see her doctor,

hoping he would prescribe her a tonic, but instead she got a lecture. 'Madame Lambert, you are exhausted. You cannot continue like this. You must have a break. What about a respite home, for a week or two, for Mr Dard? It will help you recover your strength. I know of a place, why don't I write to them?'

Reluctantly, Jane agreed. With René away she would be able to get his room painted, rearrange the furniture and complete some of the jobs she'd been putting off. The petite cabine in the garden had been plastered, ostensibly so she could use it as a painting studio, but it was full of junk. Visitors used it as a dumping ground, and bits of timber, spare parts for the lawnmower, a BBQ with only 2 legs, plant pots, bags of cement and cracked fluorescent light tubes had all been thrown in by well-meaning helpers. There wasn't much space left for painting. If she could get it cleared the petite cabine would give her the space and solitude she craved.

René wasn't keen. 'I don't want to go into a home. I like it here with you. I can help. I'll do the decorating,' he said, plaintively. Jane shook her head. She knew René didn't have the strength or the agility for any of it.

'It's better if we leave it to the professionals, René. It's only for two weeks, just while the painters are here.'

'Jeanne, are you trying to get rid of me?'

'Of course not. It's only for a short while, I promise.' A break was all she needed, just a couple of weeks.

Jane dropped René at the home on Monday, the painters arrived on Tuesday and on Wednesday morning the phone rang.

'Allo?'

'Psst, Jeanne, c'est moi!' The voice was soft and low, and whoever it was spoke in an urgent whisper that made it difficult to catch what was said. Jane moved the receiver closer to her ear. 'Allo?'

'C'est moi!' René hissed. 'You have to come and get me, it's awful, please Jeanne. I'm begging you.'

'René, the painters are here, they've turned the place upside down! What's wrong?'

'Tomorrow, please, I have to go.' René hung up before Jane could ask any more questions. His urgent pleas worried her. Perhaps something really was wrong? The only way to find out was to pay him a visit.

She drove to the nursing home the next day, half expecting to see René standing outside with a suitcase at his feet, but the drive was empty. As she pulled up outside the main entrance a forlorn looking René shuffled out to the car. Jane wound down the window.

'The doctor says I have to stay,' he said, resting his hand on the open window. 'He showed me a letter from your doctor. It said you were very tired…because of me.' René sighed, his eyes watery. 'I promise to stay, but please Jeanne, come and visit me.'

Jane went back two days later. She wheeled into the main reception area and a tall woman with shiny hair and pursed lips marched past. Her high heels clipped across the stone floor.

René nodded towards the woman. 'La directrice,' he whispered. 'We're not allowed to make phone calls. I had to sneak into her office to call you.'

Jane watched the sour faced woman stalk up the stairs without acknowledging either of them. 'Peau de vache,' Jane said. The insult raised the first smile Jane had seen from René.

He led Jane into the communal lounge, where the daily nursing staff seemed friendly enough, but only one woman bothered to reply when Jane sang out a cheery, 'Bonjour'. Most of the silent people slumped in chairs around the edge of the room ignored her.

René stumbled on a broken tile when he led Jane along the badly lit corridor that led to his bedroom. Jane fumed inwardly at the poor conditions, especially when she saw there was a light bulb missing from the ceiling outside his door. It was a hazard for someone as unsteady on his feet as René.

'How's the food?' she asked.

'Affreux,' René replied, pulling a face.

Jane vowed then and there that she would never let René be put into an old people's home on a permanent basis, no matter what the cost to her own health.

Two weeks apart gave Jane the break she needed and René the chance to reflect on his good fortune. Without Jane he almost certainly would have been confined to a nursing home, and that was a sobering thought. From then on he did his best to control his temper. Any arguments they did have were quickly rinsed away with a cup of tea and a sincere apology.

René was at his most sentimental where Jane's animals were concerned. Fauvette went missing one day and he worried out loud that she might have been kidnapped and sent to a laboratory for animal experimentation. Jane burst into tears at the thought and René rushed to apologise. 'J'ai dis les bettisses,' he said, admitting he'd been stupid to suggest such a thing. He was overjoyed to see the dog return several days later.

When the end finally came for 17-year-old Fauvette, Jane's companion for so many years, René stood over the small dog and wept. 'Please don't die,' he begged.

Six months later it was René who suggested they approach the rescue centre at Guérande to get another dog. 'The little cat misses Fauvette,' he said, artfully. The rescue centre produced Benji, another white woolly dog with trusting brown eyes, a misplaced desire to play games with Pierrot and a propensity to escape.

'She loves me already,' said René, rubbing his hands along Benji's stomach. Jane could only shake her head in disbelief.

René even made a contribution to domestic life. 'I will accompany you when you go shopping,' he announced one day. Together they drove to Auchan, a large out of town supermarket under an arching roof with aisles that went on forever. Jane grabbed a basket.

'You push and I'll collect what we need,' she said.

René turned the wheelchair into the first aisle.

'No, not this one René, we don't need anything from here.'

'Un moment,' said René, ignoring Jane's instructions. He steered her wheelchair towards a young mother with a pram and stopped to admire the baby inside. 'Is it a boy? He's handsome, n'est ce pas? Ca va mon petit?' he cooed. Jane smiled and nodded at the attractive young mum.

'It's the next aisle we need, René.'

After three more aisles and two more detours to coo over babies in prams René gave a huge sigh. 'I'm tired. I think I need to sit down. Have we finished yet?'

'René, we haven't even started!'

'Enough shopping for today,' said René and he pushed the wheelchair towards the check out. Jane was reduced to snatching things off shelves as they passed. Exasperated, she called a halt at the checkout. 'Look, you go and sit down, have a beer in Flunch and I'll join you when I've finished the shopping.'

'D'accord Jeanne,' said René, convinced he had made a major contribution to domestic life.

24 RAGING BULL

It was another two years before my next visit to Jane and René and, like Barbara, this time I was alone.

The long distance relationship in Australia had gone disastrously wrong. In an attempt to breathe life into the doomed love affair I had sent romantic poetry, ordered flowers and despatched gifts from London to Sydney. There were no arguments between us, no passion, just a soppy outpouring of understanding that was destined to lead nowhere.

It wasn't long before the fun I'd had when we met gave way to gloom. Why hasn't he called? Why hasn't he returned my call? Why only one email today? Why wasn't there a kiss at the end of his message? The answer was obvious but I chose not to see it. In a miserable swill of self-doubt (and precious little self awareness) I harangued Adam long distance about his lack of contact.

I received no declaration of love from Australia but that didn't stop me making plans to emigrate. I sold Jane's old flat in London, gave up my job and prepared to move to Sydney, where I had no work and no means of supporting myself other than with the proceeds from the sale of the flat.

When Jane sold it was a gutsy move that took months of planning. She knew that whatever success she found in France would rely on her own steely determination and resolve. I sold on a whim, to pursue a romantic dream of smoke and mirrors. In a blatant refusal to face reality, I decided not to involve Adam in my plans. I secretly hoped that when I arrived in Australia he would realise we were meant for each other, fall into my outstretched arms and all would be well.

It didn't happen.

Shortly after my arrival Adam confessed he had fallen in love with someone else, and I was dumped. I stayed, hoping he would change his mind, and I kept in touch with Jane by letter. She replied to one of my agonised outpourings with considered words of wisdom.

Well, hello my old pal Deb

I know exactly what you're going through. Men! This is my advice (which I'm going to try to follow.) Get on with your own life, enjoy your friends and food and activities and find a way to make your fortune in a self-fulfilling way. There's a lot in your life and situation that sounds great. There's a lot in my life that is great so why am I shedding tears over a man who, unless I have attractive company is thoroughly unpleasant and TOTALLY SELFISH. At our parting this morning he was trying to be conciliatory but I was in no mood for sweet words! Read on for real news…

I scraped together enough money for the return fare to England and I crept back to stay with family, eking out a precarious existence while I tried to work out what to do next. Perhaps it was the diet of fairy stories I'd been fed as a child, or the romantic fiction I had greedily consumed as a teenager that left me mystified by men. Whatever the reason, I had no idea what love really was.

Jane heard I was back and she invited me over to France. I had to decline, admitting I simply didn't have enough money to get there. A week later a letter arrived with a cheque enclosed for £250.

Dear Deb

I'm determined that you will come and see us, and that something as stupid as money will not stop you. The enclosed is on the hundred-year loan scheme. It's very good business for me because after 100 years you will owe me £250. How's that!

Lots of love

Jane

It was a typically generous offer from Jane, who had little enough money herself and I wasn't going to reject her kindness. I cashed the cheque and booked a ferry to France, vowing to pay Jane back.

Seeing her again I was reminded just how much she had managed to achieve, and against such overwhelming odds. The visit did much to lift my flagging spirits and it stopped me feeling sorry for myself.

René was more fragile than I remembered. He was in pain from arthritis in his knees and he had difficulty walking, his ill health exacerbated by problems with his heart.

'We have days full of slow activity,' said Jane, more hunched in her wheelchair but still as bright-eyed and colourful as ever.

The house was warm and inviting and the shelf of family photographs in her dining room had been added to several times. Jane was now a great grandmother several times over and she'd also discovered she had half sisters. Sandra and Nicky had tracked her down via their grandfather's trust fund and they'd been over to visit, filling Jane in with tales of the 'wicked stepmother' who had so irritated Jane when they'd spoken on the phone years before.

'They got on like a house on fire with René,' said Jane, beaming with pride.

She and I stayed up late after René had gone to bed and we talked about men. I was fixated on other people's relationships and I wondered what the glue was that kept them together.

'René's a pain in the arse,' said Jane candidly, 'but if you adopt a stray dog you are responsible for its well being.'

'Do you love him?' I asked.

'Oh yes. We've had a few 'adieu, c'est terminé,' but we're still together so I suppose that's how it's going to be.'

The next night, as we sat watching television, Jane wriggled out of her wheelchair and hauled her body onto the sofa so she could sit next to René. He ignored her struggle and did nothing to help. There was no sign of romance between them and no outward show of affection—nothing that in my Mills and Boon addled brain might constitute love—yet their relationship worked. René was full of praise and admiration for Jane, and never more so than when she stood up to him and called him to account for his bad behaviour. I took away a glimmer of understanding that love and romance were different things.

The years slipped past and a growing number of great grandchildren joined Jane's family. She and René revelled in a succession of visits from family and friends and mourned the loss of Pablo, who died, and Pierrot, who went missing and never returned. After three months they decided to adopt a kitten, Pierrette—not related to Pierrot but similar in colour with a grey coat and a pink nose. Repairs to the house continued, rotten roof tiles were replaced by watertight slate, better heating was installed in the bathroom and the grain loft was finally carpeted and decorated.

July 2004

At last I have found time to get all my news together and put it in a letter. However the reason for this opportunity is not a good one. I'm writing from a hospital bed with my right ankle in plaster and my left femur in a plaster that we call 'the wall of China.' I also had a purple forehead and a black eye which people tell me are not the right colour. I don't know because I didn't look at any stage. And all my own fault!

In early July Jane had been working in the garden, tackling weeds. She bent down to pick up a trowel and her chair wobbled on the uneven ground. She felt it slip from underneath her and there was nothing she could do to stop it. The chair tipped forwards, Jane fell out and the heavy wheelchair landed on top of her. René heard her sharp cries of pain and he went out to help. An ambulance was called, neighbours alerted and Jane was carted off to hospital with a broken right ankle and broken left femur.

With both legs in plaster she faced a prolonged stay in hospital. Friends who knew how deeply frustrating that was for her rallied to the cause. Jeannine was a regular visitor, Louise came in with a flask of tea in the afternoons, Francoise came with a pot of small change to pay for the television in Jane's hospital room and Elise brought stationery so Jane could write letters.

Now out of the intense pain region I find one or two things amusing. All the gulls, a few pigeons and sparrows and a blackbird to watch from my window and an owl that I don't know—not a barn owl. The bird that most people like is the helicopter that lands just outside on the helipad. NOISY! Otherwise I have a telly—Tour de France—and a telephone. A transfer has been arranged to a convalescent unit on Thursday. I shall leave Jean-Pierre, Didier and Tarzan with a little regret. The girl nurses are nice too but how do you fancy having your back washed by the experienced hand of a man—a Frenchman! The toll of all this on René is devastating. He doesn't eat much, smokes a lot and is tearful. Benji is lost and follows René like a shadow; Pierette occupies my bed...

René had to cope as best he could, alone apart from the animals. A young woman, Annick, came in each week to do the cleaning and she offered to do some shopping for him. Neighbours brought over pre-cooked meals, largely out of kindness to Jane, but without her there for company, René became increasingly tearful and frail. He smoked too much and ate too little until inevitably he suffered a collapse and was also admitted to hospital.

It was several weeks before Jane's plasters were replaced with plastic splints, and when she was allowed to go home, René was allowed out too. It was one of their happiest times together. Freed from the prison-like routine of hospital ward rounds and mediocre food, they felt liberated. They could drink wine at lunchtime, watch late night television, smoke cigarettes and eat nothing but bread and cheese or scorched steak and soggy vegetables. There was no one to tell them not to.

The after effects of the fall meant Jane couldn't get into bed at night, or get up in the morning without the help of a nurse. René didn't have the strength to lift her and he was too unsteady on his feet anyway. When she woke up, long before the nurse arrived to help her, Jane would switch on the television in the dining room using the remote control. There was no point calling, René was too deaf to hear. He would see the picture flicker into life from his bed in the adjoining salon and shout, 'J'arrive!' The television was his cue to make Jane a cup of tea and bring it in, along with the bedpan, which he gently slipped underneath her. It was one of the small, loving kindnesses that went unnoticed by people who only saw René as a raging bull.

Yet rage he could, and rage he did. René fought with barely contained fury at the imminent approach of death. The bright spots were when Jane had visitors. When that happened she would arrange a bbq and René would rise to the occasion. For a few hours his huge personality would expand and he'd play the genial host. Jane would glance across and see him cradling one of her great grandchildren with a broad smile on his face, and for weeks afterwards he would talk about the last set of visitors, reliving the pleasure they'd had.

'Gemma, elle est bonne gamine,' said René, remembering how Jane's granddaughter had sweetly taken his arm and led him to the toilet in a restaurant where the carpet was difficult to walk on.

'Elle est toujours aimable.'

'Yes René, she is always a very sweet girl.'

'Your friends are my friends. Your family is my family.'

'Yes, they are.'

René went into hospital for an urgent urology operation and Jane's sons, Clive and Roger, drove over to France when he came out of hospital, comforting him in a way that showed they understood the humiliation a man like René might suffer. But life wasn't the same for him from then on. Each day there was something else he couldn't manage; a drive he declined, a walk he chose not to take, an urgent trip to the bathroom he didn't quite make. Worsening arthritis, a weak heart, increasing deafness and the need to pee every fifteen minutes made life miserable for René.

Jane's granddaughter, Abby, was visiting with her husband, James, and their three children at the height of summer in 2006. René thought Jane's three granddaughters were beautiful girls and he loved the company of 'les petits'. Spoon feeding a child or giving a baby a bottle were simple pleasures he could still enjoy. He'd been poorly for a couple of days and twice he'd fallen over. Each time Abby or James helped him to his feet. René responded well to Abby's gentle manner. 'Elle m'aime beaucoup - she loves me so much,' he said, in typical fashion.

Jane was worried it wasn't much of a holiday for the children so she persuaded Abby to take them to the beach for the day while she stayed at home to look after René. The plan was for them to all go out for a meal together that night.

'Do you feel well enough to come?' Jane asked.

'No,' he said, 'but you go.'

Jane left René with a tray of things to eat and when they came back later that night she found him sitting on the edge of his bed, his arm in a sling. 'What happened?' she asked. 'I fell. Francoise called in, she found me. She bandaged it.'

'Do you want to go to hospital?'

'No, not to hospital Jeanne.'

'Can I get you anything? '

'Non merci.'

Jane placed a glass of water by the side of his bed and wished René goodnight. The next morning, when she went to check on him, his body was cold.

Jane's last gift to René was to make sure he died at home, and not in a hospital bed surrounded by strangers.

25 RALLYING

The exhaustion of looking after René was replaced by a sense of loss so acute Jane wondered how she would get through it. She wasn't even sure she wanted to. In spite of their tempestuous relationship, and the considerable work involved in looking after him, the loss for Jane was enormous.

'He was the love of my life,' she said, simply.

Jane's grandchildren and great grandchildren visited from England and friends and neighbours rallied, all helping to pull Jane back from the brink of depression. Jeannine and Robert, Francoise, Jean Yves and Lucien called regularly. Privately, they all thought Jane was better off without René, Jeannine especially.

The prolonged spell in hospital left Jane unable to manage on her own. A succession of nurses called day and night to help get Jane in and out of bed and Annick came every few days to do the cleaning.

Jane hated the lack of independence, yet, in spite of everything, there was still the garden. Over the previous two years, during her stay in hospital and later, when René had been so unwell, there hadn't been much time for gardening.

Nature had progressed in its own sweet way and the results weren't that different from the way Jane might have done it—apart from the bindweed that had crept across the flowerbeds. Allowed to wander unchecked it had flowered, splashing white into the showy mix of red and yellow dahlias. She peered into the tangled mass and there, nestled in the midst of the creeping weed, was a little plum tree. It had taken root when she'd thrown out a plum stone years

226

before.

Roses bloomed in spite of being covered in black spot and the lavender Jane had planted three years earlier was now a fragrant hedge. Everywhere she looked, herbs tumbled onto the concrete paths. She wheeled through a carpet of greenery, releasing the scent of crushed mint, rosemary and thyme as she slowly passed.

The branches of the peach tree René loved were weighed down with sweet smelling, succulent fruit, and the apple tree was so laden with fruit it looked like a cartoon; Disney's Sleeping Beauty come to life. Like the house, her garden was full of objects that were useful and would take too much trouble and energy to put away only to get them out again.

Amongst the verdant life were clumps of gravel, plant pots, dog bowls, Tupperware, children's toys, an old laundry basket, a dustpan and brush, bags of straw, a sand pit, garden gnomes, an old trowel. It all had a use.

That night Jane spent several hours collecting a bucket full of snails. She gave them to Jeannine. 'A present, for your chickens,' she said.

There was no point moping. She bought a rose, Nostalgie, and planted it in memory of René then she cleared the furniture from his room and had floorboards laid on the ground floor, replacing the stone and lino that had been there from the start. She also insulated and decorated her own bedroom. Outside she repainted the fence in the back garden a rich black colour, using spent oil from the garage that they happily gave away for free.

I visited Jane the following summer, still single but finally standing on my own. The failed romance hadn't put me off Australia and I had gone back. After a period of hard work and dogged persistence I had built up enough work as a freelance journalist to earn a living. I wrote features for interiors magazines, touring some of the most beautiful houses in the wealthier suburbs of Sydney. It taught me an important lesson—no amount of money spent on interior design can replicate the warmth that is apparent when a house is filled with love.

Jane's house, for all its quirky eccentricity, was far more attractive than many of the million dollar mansions I was writing about.

During my visit Jane's next-door neighbour, Jeannine, called in to say hello. I'd met Jeannine many times and she was an easy woman to warm to, open, friendly and fiercely protective of Jane.

'René was good company but frankly, a lot of work,' she said, standing behind Jane's chair and addressing me in French, over the top of Jane's head. 'She looks good, no? Better since René, don't you think?'

Jane sighed. She knew her next-door neighbour meant well, after all Jeannine had picked Jane off the floor more times than she could remember.

'But she's still so stubborn,' Jeannine continued. 'There are days when she's in pain all over but she won't call the doctor.'

Jane raised her eyes towards the ceiling. 'Exhibit A,' she muttered and we both laughed.

'Je l'estime comme si elle etais ma mere,' said Jeannine suddenly. Her voice wavered as she confessed the depth of her affection for Jane. 'Elle est formidable,' she added gruffly. She turned to Jane and spoke with mock solemnity to suppress the emotion that threatened to overwhelm her. 'You have to rely on your girlfriends now. No more boyfriends!'

Jane nodded, her eyes gleaming with mischievous delight.

Driving became more hazardous and getting in and out of the car more of a struggle. The accidents were minor—a scraped bumper, a cracked mirror—but each one knocked her confidence. Pam came to visit and Jane took her out for the day, Pam sitting bolt upright in the passenger seat, willing Jane to concentrate. It was a warm afternoon and she had seen Jane's head dip forward a couple of times.

The driver behind suddenly sounded his horn.

'Why is he hooting?' said Jane.

'You've drifted over the white line.'

'Nonsense, he just wants to get past. Some people have no patience.'

Pam was a bundle of nerves, flinching at every corner, twitching when the car came too close to the side of the road. Jane couldn't help but notice.

'What on earth is the matter with you Pam?'

'We're almost in the ditch.'

'Rubbish, it only looks that way.'

'Trust me Jane, we are almost in the ditch!'

They got home and drove into Jane's driveway where, with a gentle nudge, Jane knocked down the post box. Pam silently vowed never to get in a car with her again.

After Pam left Jane made a list of things to do. It included 'practise driving', but no amount of practise was enough. After several more near misses Jane lost her confidence completely. The car languished in the garage and Jane went shopping every week with her pal, Muriel, who helped haul her into her car then loaded the wheelchair into the boot. Lucien charged the battery of Jane's car every month just in case, but the discovery of a wasp's nest under the bonnet signalled the end. She eventually sold the car to a one-legged Chadian, who crashed it on the way home.

Bit by bit Jane recovered her strength and she dispensed with the night nurse. Instead of being put to bed at nine o'clock she went to bed as late as she liked. It made a world of difference. Now she only needed help getting up in the morning. Seed catalogues with pictures of spring bulbs and tender young vegetables held the promise of a brighter future, and they cheered her up and helped her through the worst of winter.

When Jeanine popped in for a cup of tea a few days before Christmas Jane called her into the sitting room. 'Look at this,' she said. 'Just look how beautiful that is.' She pointed towards a potted amaryllis, which that morning had unfurled a single, deep red bloom. On the bleakest winter morning, when the wind was howling outside and the sky blanketed in grey, the beauty of an individual flower had lifted her spirits.

Jane wasn't convinced she would see eighty but her body—and her family—thought otherwise.

'Mum? It's Jenny. We're going to throw a party for your eightieth.'

'Must you?'

'Yes. Don't worry, we'll organise it, you won't have to do a thing.'

Jenny swung into action, enlisting the help of her oldest daughter Gemma, a social researcher. Together they contacted Clive, Annabel, Roger and Jenny's twin sister Nicky, who used to live in Holland and had moved back to the UK. They agreed to arrange the party in Jane's back garden, on the last bank holiday in August. The next generation down were alerted and they made plans to spend their summer holidays in France, bringing Jane's great grandchildren, seven of them at the last count.

Jenny handed out jobs; sourcing champagne, sending invites, preparing food, bringing chairs, arranging transport and booking campsites. Jewellery designer Annabel's job was to find a suitable birthday cake so she went to a cake shop in Ealing Broadway and leafed through a book of designs. The main theme seemed to be a disappointing dark brown chocolate.

'What other colours have you got?' Annabel asked.

'Pale blue and pale pink are quite popular. There's always white of course.'

'What about red?'

'Red?'

'Yes, pillar-box red. Mum's a Leo. She'll love it. I'd like a huge cake with red icing…and swags!' said Annabel, warming to the theme. 'Eight swags around the outside, one for each decade, with edible flowers in blues, pinks, reds and yellows.'

On the bank holiday weekend, the juggernaut of Jane's family made its way to France, many of them heading to a campsite in nearby St Marc which Jane had scouted out earlier in the year—a wooded spot with direct access to the beach through a tunnel under the road, plus a swimming pool and tennis and badminton courts. It was perfect for the little ones.

Gemma and her husband, Ben, commandeered a corner of the campsite under a bank of trees and they pitched their tent with toddlers Max and Charlie, the latter a diminutive clown who made everyone laugh. Gemma's sister, Abby, her husband, James, and children Tim, Alex and Kirsty joined them. The only girl in five cousins, Kirsty had no trouble holding her own amongst the boys. As cute as a button, she was clearly destined for the stage.

Third sister Kate, another teacher, arrived with her boyfriend, Grant, from Pretoria. The 'Dutch lot' camped too—Nicky's children Somiah, who brought her boyfriend, Robbie, and Ilya, with his daughter Isis. Roger, Jane's youngest came with daughters Becky and Vicky, Becky with adorable 10 month-old Riley in tow. Dorothy Lamour lookalike Vicky—a brilliant merchant banker—arrived in an Audi with her fellow merchant banker boyfriend, Adrian, and they pitched their tent too. Jenny and Tim camped in the back garden and Clive, Annabel and Xavier slept in the grain loft. The only person who couldn't make it was Nicky, who sadly was too ill to travel.

Cousins who hadn't seen each for years were reacquainted. There was Jenny and Tim's daughter, Katy, who worked as a teacher and her boyfriend, Grant, an accountant. There was Somaya's boyfriend, Robbie, who worked as a gardener in season and a builder out of season, on Amsterdam's floating houses. He was captivated by Jane's garden.

There was Annabel's son, Xavier, once called Galeesh from the story about the King of France's daughter, who ran away with the fairies. His name was changed from Galeesh to Xavier when he started suffering from narcolepsy. The sleep condition mysteriously resolved itself soon after. The name Xavier comes from the Basque place name Etcheberria, which means *new house*. Xavier's father Patrick—who had no idea what the new name meant—promptly gave his son a house.

Annabel's talent for making exquisite jewellery had flourished in the years since her mum had moved to France and her mane of hair was now dyed the rich colour of boiled beetroot.

Grown ups sat under the trees chatting, drinking wine, champagne and ginger beer, while small children played contentedly in the sand pit. The smallest child, Riley, pottered about the garden and he quietly made friends with Benji. Games overcame any language barrier with Ilya's daughter Isis, who spoke only Dutch and was meeting her English relatives for the first time, but there was little that could overcome Ilya's sombre mood after a spell in Afghanistan.

Food came and went then came and went again, a procession of burnt sausages, burgers, chicken wings, sausage rolls, salad, fruit puddings and cake.

It turned out to be the perfect party, on a perfect summer's day. Jane quaffed 'Mumm' champagne and drifted through the hot afternoon surrounded by children, grandchildren and great-grandchildren. She thrilled them all by wearing, quite by chance, a cotton shirt in the same colours as her birthday cake—pillarbox red with small blue flowers.

At some point during that long afternoon, which slipped unnoticed into evening, Jane's good friend Pam rang and sang *Happy Birthday*, which prompted a group rendition in the garden, Jenny's beautiful voice carrying across the fields. Neighbours popped in to say hello but they didn't stay long. They'd had their own celebrations with Jane the week before. This was family time.

Jane's children made her a collage of photographs, from the time when she'd been a small girl, and Annabel made a birthday card, painted with a tree root.

Happy Birthday Mum.
Grandma to so many.
Time to put a story down,
About your journey to this town,
And which peculiar strange fruit
Was it that created your new root.

Jane's children, grandchildren and great grandchildren all had a great time and Jane overheard one of them remark, 'Isn't it fun, meeting up like this? We should do it more often.' She couldn't help smiling. The next time would probably be her funeral.

Before the visitors left there was just time for a quick trip to the campsite then the local supermarket with Abby and James, who had thoughtfully driven over in a car Jane could get into. They had lunch in 'Flunch', where Jane and René always used to go, and bought presents for the little ones.

Jane was moved by the show of so much affection. An only child, she had been raised by a single parent and spent most of her childhood in the company of adults, only discovering she had half sisters when she was in her mid sixties. She had been forcibly separated from her own children when they were placed in separate foster homes after polio struck. It took years to get them back.

The party in France was an antidote to all of that. Initially reluctant, Jane was glad in the end that she had been persuaded to celebrate, she'd always wanted a big family.

'If only René had lived to be a part of it,' she said. 'He always loved a good party.'

26 APPROACHING THE END

Death holds no fear for Jane. She felt René move through the house about a week after he died. A sensation of warmth enveloped her for a moment then he was gone.

She's seen the old lady who used to live in her house too. Early one morning, just after she woke up, when she was still lying in bed, she saw a woman standing at the back of her wheelchair. The smiling apparition had full cheeks and hair pulled back into a chignon. She was looking across at Jane with quiet approval. There was a faint family resemblance to Madame Lagueux, only the smiling apparition wasn't as tall. It was hardly worth checking, Jane knew who it had to be, but she asked Jeannine all the same. The description matched that of Madame Lagueux's mother, the woman who had originally lived in Jane's house.

Jane took another tumble out of her wheelchair in June 2010. Her knee buckled under and she broke her right femur, heralding another prolonged spell in hospital. I went out to visit when she was back at home and we sat in her dining room, chatting about the future. There was an envelope pinned to the notice board above her head, with instructions written on the outside: *Directions a suivre après le deces de Jane Lambert. Things to do after the death of Jane Lambert.*

'Flu would be a good way to go, don't you think?' she said. 'It used to be called the old people's friend. Why are we so obsessed with prolonging life? So we've got a better chance of getting Alzheimer's or bowel cancer? There comes a point when you have to question the viability of keeping someone like me alive.'

Her eyes took on their familiar glint and she smiled. 'I want my ashes scattered in the back garden. That way I can keep an eye on things and make sure no one messes it up. Did your fork just break? Mind that spade, you don't want to have an accident.' She lifted her head and laughed with impish delight at the thought of coming back to haunt prospective new owners if they dared to dig up her precious garden and replace it with concrete pavers. If there's any chance of coming back to check on the garden after she dies, Jane will be there.

Jeannine called in while I was there. She was surprised to learn Jane had bought the champagne for her funeral and stored it in the cupboard under the stairs. She was even more upset at the prospect of a back yard burial and the promise of Jane hanging around after death. She refused to go along with the plan, shaking her head vigorously as she folded her arms.

'Ah non! Ca va pas! I am not putting you in the garden. I will put you in the sea or in the marshes, but I refuse to put you in the garden. I will see you every morning and night. Ah non, non, non.' Jeannine made Jane promise to make other arrangements.

Jane smiled. Her mind was made up long ago. 'The French are thinking of bringing in a law forbidding it, but my children will know what to do,' she told me later. 'They'll replace the ashes in the urn with soot from a bonfire, or maybe a trowel full of earth, and scatter what remains of me across garden. It will make a perfect last resting place. Until then I'm going to eat what I like, drink what I like and smoke if I want to. Why not? I can't have long to go.'

Life in Maca has changed. There's a house being built in the field at the back of Jane's house and planning permission granted for another beside it. Donges has grown as the oil refinery and the shipbuilding industry in nearby St Nazaire expand. It's no longer enough to write Jane's name on a letter, the post office demands a street number now. Jane sighs. 'The things I left behind are catching up with me.'

Aldo, a lovely postman who often took Jane's parcels to the post office, has retired. He was taken on a tour of the villages and hamlets where he used to deliver and people came out in force to wish him well. Lucien is in his mid eighties now and still going strong. When he became a grandfather he bought a Shetland pony for the children to ride. His wife, Therese, died of pancreatic cancer and was mourned by all of Maca.

Francoise and Jean Yves have both retired and are still living over the road. They call in for an aperitif and help with shopping, dog washing and anything else that might need doing. Francoise is as elegant as ever, with manicured nails, pressed jeans and neatly cropped hair.

Jeannine's husband, Robert, suffered a stroke, which made walking and talking difficult, and he and Jeannine gave up on the goat, geese and lambs they sometimes used to keep. He died a couple of years ago. Jeannine still lives next door and she suffers pain in her knees and feet, but she always finds things to laugh about.

Alain, the man up the road who loved dogs and hunting, ended up living in a caravan when his house became so dilapidated it was no longer habitable. A lovely character, admired by many, his thirst eventually got the better of him. Over two hundred people attended his funeral.

The gardening gang has been disbanded. Romain, who loved to chew the fat man to man with René, bought a pizzeria and still visits occasionally. Morgan turned into an academic and Angelique is married and expecting her first baby. They've been replaced over the years by a succession of others.

Saeed won René's heart in spite of being '...a little bit Arab', and he was a great help until he slipped a disk lifting his three-year-old daughter out of the car and was forced to give up gardening. There was an unemployed lad for a while, a sturdy boy, good at telling a weed from a plant but not a long-term prospect. Visitors are always willing to pitch in. Jane wonders if that's how she lost six hollyhocks, an over enthusiastic machine minded helper, weeding with the hedge trimmer. Now there's Monsieur Mercier, who often forgets what he planted and digs it back up again.

The house is quieter without René although just as colourful. Ageing posters of butterflies, crabs and lobsters still hang on the walls in the ochre coloured kitchen, and a plastic covered tablecloth, glossy with fruit as vibrant as an underwater scene from the Great Barrier Reef, covers the table in the yellow dining room. A green and yellow striped curtain hangs at the door next to a spinning mobile of doves and rainbow stripes. Pale pink cushions cover chairs, the veranda is mint green and the bedroom strawberry pink. Posters of amphibians and reptiles hang on green walls in the bathroom beneath a ceiling painted Matisse blue.

Clothes on an open rack in Jane's bedroom suggest sunny days spent outdoors. Trousers in red, aqua, magenta, olive green, taupe and mustard yellow hang beside a blouse with orange hibiscus flowers, another in peacock blue, a third in the striped colours of a rainbow.

The cupboards are crammed with things that might be useful, old shoes, bits of broken sewing machine, light bulbs, wire, pieces of material, foam rubber. One carrier bag holds bits of a wooden puzzle that aren't all there. Jane thinks she might turn them into a sculpture. Wrapping paper, tracing paper, exercise books, trousers that need darning, poles from a shelving unit thrown away years before, knitting wool, old socks, empty tins, floppy hats, bubble wrap and clothes visitors could wear for gardening are all jammed into the cupboard under a nest of baby spiders. She opens bags and boxes, searching for a photograph she wants to show me, marvelling at what she finds.

'Oh look, I've got some more champagne.'

'So that's where the pegs went.'

'That white cardboard will do for making a Valentine's Day card.'

'What's that bauble doing there? It should go in the bag of Christmas decorations.'

Jane finds a credit card she lost weeks before. 'Maybe if I start looking for the credit card I'll find the photograph,' she muses. Eventually she gives up on the search and pushes it all back into the cupboard.

Jeannine pops in later and finds us trying to stuff the seat of Jane's wheelchair with foam. It's become uncomfortable, at times painful, and sometimes Jane can't make it around the supermarket without stifling a scream.

'Can I help?' Jeannine asks.

'I need to raise the sides to take the pressure off the base of my spine,' says Jane.

We do our best but in the end it's given up as a lost cause and we sit and watch the Tour de France on television, something that ranks alongside the Chelsea Flower Show on Jane's list of all time favourite television viewing. The cyclists pass a magnificent chateau and Jeannine laughs.

'There you go Jane, you can give me a chateau if you like.'

Jane makes a mental note. She'll paint Jeannine a picture of a chateau, viewed through an arch to signify the welcome Jeannine has always extended to her. Deep in the cupboard is an old calendar with a turret in one scene that's exactly the shape she needs for the chateau. She'll have a look for it later, she tells me.

Jane is noticeably more hunched in her chair. She's had her hair cut short and let it revert to a natural snow-white. Her head drops, as if she can't summon the strength to raise it, but when she does the mega watt smile is as powerful as ever. There's a small collection of books in the dining room that reflect Jane's interests—*Food for Free* by Richard Mabey, *Fairies of the Trees*, the *Collins Gem Guide to Insects, Fruits, Nuts and Berries* and the *Observer Book of Trees*. In French there's *Voir les Papilons, and Les Oiseaux*. And for the many small children who visit there are *Just So Stories*, the *Tale of Mr Jeremy Fisher* and the *Tale of Johnny Town Mouse*.

Benji, more woolly sheep than dog, is not the brightest. He's been known to try and bury a biscuit in the dining room floor but he adores Jane and the feeling is mutual. Pierette, her impossibly beautiful Siamese cross, sleeps in an old wicker tray on top of a shelving unit and occasionally condescends to be stroked and fed.

Open cartons of dog food and cat food are simply dropped onto the floor for them to chase around. It's easier than trying to decant the contents into a bowl.

The west-facing garden, once an empty field scorched by sunlight, is now a paradise of colour and texture, with height, structure and welcome pockets of shade.

Sometimes the catalpa tree blooms, sometimes it doesn't. Jane doesn't mind. She loves the sun shining through its big leaves, lighting up the top of the garden. A cherry tree bought cheaply from the local supermarket stands over six metres tall now, with a spread almost as wide. The apple trees Clive supplied are mature and productive, so much so that the Cox needs to be propped. Everyone in Maca reaps the rewards of the harvest.

Sadly the magnificent peach tree, which René adored and which just appeared one day, a dieu donné or gift from God, is dying. No matter, it will make room for a larger seating area. At the top of the garden is a James Greave, a mountain ash next to the catalpa to attract birds and a buddleah to attract butterflies. A new weeping willow beside the pond soaks up excess moisture and the damson tree beyond it produces pots and pots of jam.

Roses are everywhere. There's Rosa rugosa to remind Jane of Roger and Rosa astronomia for Clive, who once published a book on Christian astrology. It's the closest she could get. Gemma has a pink rose, Rebecca a red pink variety and of course there's 'nostalgie' for René. Annabel has a white hydrangea. 'It needs a bit of TLC,' says Jane, quietly.

The unruly yellow climber that sprawls over a central arch has an echo in an old yellow rose at the top of the garden. An early flowerer, it heralds a profusion of blooms. A Dutch rose, Weischenblau, its pink blooms faintly tinged with blue, smells of lily of the valley. Planted outside the back door, Jane encourages it to ramble over the back of the house.

The passion fruit vine still clings to the cabine wall, self-seeding sweet peas clamber up the trunk of the peach tree and geraniums sprawl under the Blenheim Orange. Grape hyacinth, sedum, fusain, marigolds, canicule, alyssum saxatile, variegated sage and euphorbia provide ground cover.

Pierette pushes her nose into banks of sweet smelling lavender, mint and rosemary. A curry bush sprawls near the 'fosse septique', where other shallow rooted plants such as rhubarb and blue geranium flourish. Eunonymous, smelling faintly of vanilla, flowers in winter. Mexican orange, bright showy dahlias, laurel, lichen, red hot pokers, hollyhocks, iris—the list goes on and on. Somewhere in there are potatoes, the well known 'sprouting at the bottom of the bag' variety. Rather than throw them out Jane planted them.

In autumn the garden is full of whispers. The wind brushes against fat rose hips, papery sweet peas, poppies and thistles. Dried flower heads are laden with seeds and balanced on brittle stems. Jane will only cut them down when she's sure they've had a chance to sow next year's crop. If there's any doubt she'll harvest the seeds herself and scatter them on the ground.

'Do you know, fifty per cent of the world's plants are endangered,' she says, reaching precariously across a patch of pelargonium to tuck another tulip bulb into the ground. 'If we don't do something to save them we'll end up totally reliant on big business and genetically modified hybrids. Nature does it far better than we can, all we have to do is give her a helping hand.'

She points out that commercially produced tomatoes are designed to withstand an impact of twenty kilometres an hour. They can fall from a height of two metres and not be dented. 'But what do they taste like? And what chemicals have been used to grow them? That doesn't seem to matter,' she says. Her tomato seeds for next year's crop are ready and waiting in the veranda.

Jane still hates the 'ghastly winter' when she can easily get depressed and acknowledges she made a mistake thinking French winters would be milder. Come spring though, she's back out in the garden, planting peas and broad beans, trusting to luck to see if she can outwit the slugs and snails. She moves them around, hides them amongst other plants. Friends stay in touch and visit regularly—Pam spent a week with Jane the year after she turned eighty, helping to weed the unruly plot.

If Jane takes a cup of tea outside she still flings the tea bag onto the garden, a habit she's had for years. It might end up tangled in a rosemary bush, or caught in the branches of an apple tree, where it will dangle until it drops to the ground. Wherever it lands, it will gradually decay and improve the soil. Old cardboard boxes are left to do the same.

Jane lives life at a slower pace than the rest of us; she has no choice. It means she often sees things the rest of us miss, like cuckoo pint flowering in ditches, the first camellia bud of winter unfurling, the smallest lizard sunning itself on a rock. She's good at paying attention and learning from what she sees.

The swallows never came back. Owls that used to nest in Alain's chimney and fly over her garden at night to land on the garage roof have gone. She gave up watching for the babies' heads to pop up when the parents came back with food. The nightingale that perched in the garden, singing its heart out day and night, has gone too. Happily there are some survivors. The bats are still there, although fewer, and so are the blackbirds, song thrushes, robins, wrens, magpies and jays that steal the cherries. Gliding and swirling overhead are buzzards, the male a beautiful silver with yellow eyes and legs.

Jane's got the answer to the house being built at the back. She's going to plant a small strip of woodland at the top of the garden; not just one variety of tree either—diversity is the key.

'The Breton pines around here had processional caterpillars and they sprayed them. Birds ate the insects and suddenly we had no swallows. If they hadn't planted so many of the same tree in the first place they wouldn't have had such a problem,' she mutters.

The miniature strip of woodland will also correct a mistake made many years earlier, when the fence was erected in the wrong place. 'I'll plant a wisteria, the blue will help lend distance.' There's always something else to be done in the garden, and never enough time.

Jane is approaching eighty-four now. Despite the lightness of spirit that belies her age, she knows she's reaching the end. She's hoping that when she goes the house will be sold to someone else who is disabled, or someone of small stature. 'Such people often get forgotten,' she says. 'Nothing's ever at the right height and this house would be perfect.'

POSTSCRIPT

I never saw a wild thing
Sorry for itself.
A small bird will drop frozen from a bough
Without ever having felt sorry for itself.
    DH Lawrence

Jane has learnt to live with the frustration of muscles that won't respond and limbs that won't move. If she has to operate at a snail's pace in order to achieve her goal, that's what she will do. She is 'drenched with purpose' as poet Thom Gunn put it.

I marvel at what Jane has managed to achieve. She went in search of love and adventure at an age when most people are content to slip quietly into retirement. She threw herself into another culture, learnt a foreign language, made new friends, converted a rundown shack into a comfortable home and created a garden of rare beauty. Along the way she met the love of her life. Love, not money, drove her every move.

My friendship with this beautiful woman has taught me that freezing damsons before you cook them will make the stones easier to extract, ginger beer tastes better when you add a dash of gin to it and even if a peach looks mottled and discoloured on the outside it might still taste sweet and juicy on the inside. I've learnt that if I wake up in the middle of the night and find a full moon shining it's worth stepping outside, worth taking a moment to feel the cool light spill onto my face and watch it bathe the garden in midnight magic. I accept that slugs and snails might eat half of the vegetables I grow, it's enough to know I'll get the other half—better that than poison the soil with chemicals.

I've learnt it's ok to live with disorder, my pens don't have to line up and the ironing can wait. So what if the cushions don't match or the grout in the bathroom tiles is grey? It doesn't matter. On my last visit to see Jane, half an hour before I was due to leave, a friend spilt red wine over my white trousers. I whipped them off, used Jane's remedy of adding white wine and the stain magically disappeared.

I realise life is worth living to the full, no matter how challenging it might seem, and it's worth finding a fulfilling way of earning your own living, single or not. Find something you love doing and give yourself to it. There's no point being half hearted about life, or love.

Thanks to Jane I finally understand the difference between love and romance. I know the search for perfection is doomed to failure and I've stopped looking for the knight in shining armour who will rescue me from my forlorn state of singledom. Once I did that I found an unexpected mate, someone I can have some fun with. Thanks to Jane I know there's fun to be had at any age.

Jane has taught me that it's never too late to embark on an adventure, to see what's around the corner, meet new people, make new friends and maybe, just maybe, meet the love of your life. Anything can happen.

Jane has taught me many things, but the gift I treasure most is the ability to slow down and appreciate the quiet things in life. She has taught me to see beauty, wherever I'm prepared to look for it.

When Jane dies she will leave a small patch of this planet greener than she found it and many people richer for having known her.

Her legacy is a gift I will treasure.

ABOUT THE AUTHOR

Deb Hunt grew up in a Gloucestershire village and spent many years working in London as a PR consultant, writer, event manager, actor and theatre producer. She moved to Australia in 1999 and worked as a journalist with *Australian House & Garden* magazine. After several years flitting back and for between England and Australia she took a job with the Royal Flying Doctor Service and spent three years in Broken Hill. She now lives in Sydney with her partner, Clyde, and Maggie, their domesticated dingo.

Made in the USA
Charleston, SC
15 December 2013